Contents

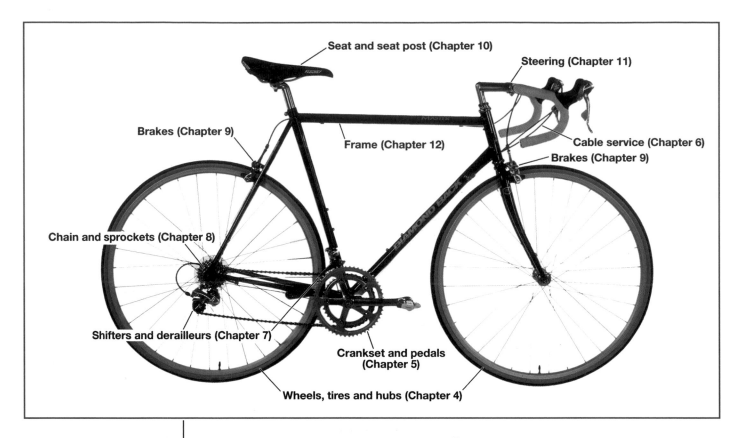

Seat and seat post (Chapter 10)

Steering (Chapter 11)

Brakes (Chapter 9)

Frame (Chapter 12)

Cable service (Chapter 6)

Brakes (Chapter 9)

Chain and sprockets (Chapter 8)

Shifters and derailleurs (Chapter 7)

Crankset and pedals (Chapter 5)

Wheels, tires and hubs (Chapter 4)

The Haynes Bicycle Book

by Bob Henderson

The Haynes Repair Manual
for maintaining and repairing your bike

Haynes Publishing Group
Sparkford Nr Yeovil
Somerset BA22 7JJ England

Haynes North America, Inc
861 Lawrence Drive
Newbury Park
California 91320 USA

Acknowledgements

We are grateful for the help of many individuals and companies in the production of this book. These include Access Marketing, Bicycle Parts Pacific, the Cannondale Corporation, Bob Seals of Cool Tool, Giro Sport Design, Headland Bicycle Accessories, Onza, Park Tool Company, Pedro's, SDG USA, Syntace, and Western States Imports (Diamond Back bicycles and Avenir accessories).

Special thanks go out to Wendy Henderson and Chris Hofmann for their mechanical skills, Michael Thomas and the rest of the crew at Michael's Bicycles in Newbury Park, CA, Eileen Fore and Kent Reppert II (page layout and graphics), Mickee Ferrell (cover design), Bobby Henderson (test pilot), Mike Stubblefield and Janis McCormick for the use of their Eisentrauts, Robert C. Henderson (Schwinn Continental), Sue Henderson (Centurion Cavaletto and babysitting services), Al Seyle and Jay Storer (photographic assistance) and Rob Maddox and Lisa Baltrushes (models). Without all of your help this book would not have been possible.

© **Haynes North America, Inc. 1995**

With permission from J.H. Haynes & Co. Ltd.

A book in the Haynes Automotive Repair Manual Series

Printed in the U.S.A.

ISBN 1 56392 137 5

Library of Congress Catalog Card Number 95-79396

While every attempt is made to ensure that the information in this manual is correct, no liability can be accepted by the authors or publishers for loss, damage or injury caused by any errors in, or omissions from, the information given.

95-192

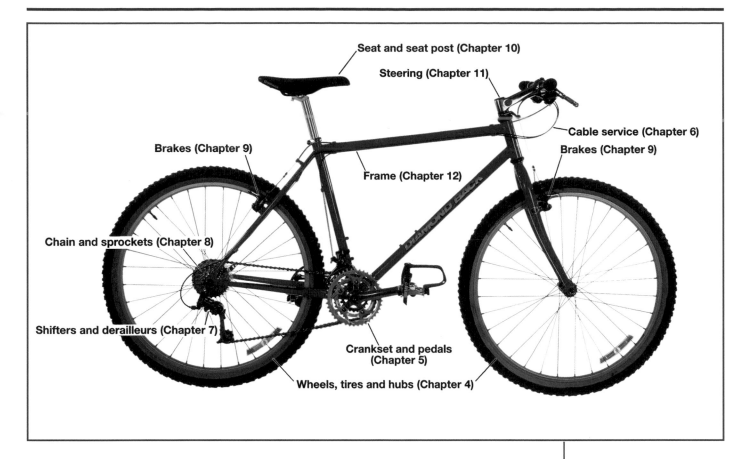

Seat and seat post (Chapter 10)

Steering (Chapter 11)

Cable service (Chapter 6)

Brakes (Chapter 9)

Brakes (Chapter 9)

Frame (Chapter 12)

Chain and sprockets (Chapter 8)

Shifters and derailleurs (Chapter 7)

Crankset and pedals (Chapter 5)

Wheels, tires and hubs (Chapter 4)

Introduction

Bicycles are fun. Sure, they're used as a primary form of transportation in many countries, by police in some urban areas, raced by some of the world's top athletes for serious money and have even been used by bank robbers to make quick getaways in crowded cities. But for the most part, bikes are used for recreation and exercise. It's hard *not* to have fun on a bike!

Take a few moments to reminisce about your first bike. Most of us will probably recall memories of teetering down the sidewalk, relying on our training wheels to keep us upright, or our parents running along side of us shouting encouraging praises as we learned to balance on two wheels.

As we got a little older, our bikes helped us achieve our independence (if we got our homework done on time!). Our bikes enabled us to get to our friend's house or to the local field or fire trail to put each others skills to the test. When they broke we became educated in our first attempts at mechanical repairs.

To those of you reading this who are old enough to have to think back to those days, realizing it has been quite a few years since, perhaps cycling plays an even greater role in your life. The fun quotient hasn't diminished one bit *and* you're getting the exercise you need, provided you ride about three times a week. On top of that, and possibly the best aspect of biking, is the reduction of stress that you're bound to feel as soon as you climb aboard your bike. It's like magic - a few turns of the cranks, a few drops of sweat - before you know it you've forgotten about the pressures at work, that horrible traffic jam you were trapped in, taxes, politics, crime, etc. Your mind empties out all of those unpleasant things and you start to feel good again, even to the point of regaining some of the innocence of youth. Or it least it feels that way!

Bikes serve us well, so they deserve some of our attention to keep them running right. And, like any mechanical object, sooner or later something will break or become out of adjustment. This is no cause for discouragement - bikes are fun, so maintaining and fixing them should be fun, too. It's just another part of cycling, and can be just as relaxing as riding them as long as you know what you're doing.

That's where this book comes in. It has been designed to help just about anyone repair just about any problem on just about any kind of bike. Beginners, novices and experts alike can use this manual to keep their bikes in top shape. If you're a beginner, consider this book your "training wheels." If you're a novice mechanic, think of it as your "independence" - from being dependent on the bike shop. If you're a fairly experienced bike mechanic, it'll still be useful as a source of reference, offering reassuring glimpses into components or systems that you may not be very familiar with.

Most modern bicycles are actually quite simple to maintain and repair, provided each step is performed in a careful, deliberate manner. A considerable amount of time and money can be saved and much knowledge can be gained by taking on these tasks yourself. This will give you a great sense of satisfaction - not only because you saved a bunch of money and your bike wasn't tied up for a couple of days in a shop, but simply because working on bicycles is enjoyable.

The procedures illustrated throughout the book are general in nature; most bikes are very similar to each other. However, where necessary, specific differences in component design are pointed out to help you complete each procedure safely and properly. Included are chapters on setting up your bike to fit your body, maintaining and cleaning your bike, troubleshooting, and chapters on repairing, replacing and adjusting every part of the modern bicycle. In short, everything you need to know to successfully maintain and repair your bike and ensure your safety and enjoyment while participating in this great sport.

How to use this manual

The manual is divided into chapters. Each chapter is subdivided into sections, some of which consist of consecutively numbered paragraphs (usually referred to as "Steps," since they're normally part of a procedure). If the material is basically informative in nature, rather than a step-by-step procedure, the paragraphs aren't numbered.

The sections are consecutively numbered, but where differences in a particular component design exist, the section will be subdivided into as many subsections as necessary to keep each component design in order. These subsections will have letters following the section numbers. For example, Section 4 may cover three different variations on a certain component; the first design covered would be under 4a, the second design 4b, and the third design being 4c. Oc-casionally this is carried a step further, where there are sub-groupings of each particular design. In this case, the subsections would be separated by a period and a number, like this: 4a.1, 4a.2, 4b.1, 4b.2, and so on. There are some sections that are even broken down to another level, where the period and number is followed by a letter. This may seem confusing right now, but it won't as soon as you immerse yourself into a procedure. It's the easiest way to separate the many different component designs found on the bicycles you're likely to encounter.

Photographs are sequentially numbered within a Chapter and iden-tified by a number in a blue dot on the photo itself. The text will identify when there is an associated photo with the reference **"Photo 1"**, **"Photo 2"**, etc.

The terms **"Note,"** **"Caution,"** and **"Warning"** are used throughout the book with a specific purpose in mind - to attract the reader's atten-tion. A **"Note"** simply provides infor-mation required to properly complete a procedure or information which will make the procedure easier to under-stand. A **"Caution"** outlines a special procedure or special steps which must be taken when completing the procedure where the Caution is found. Failure to pay attention to a Caution can result in damage to the compo-nent being repaired or the tools being used. A **"Warning"** is included where personal injury can result if the in-structions aren't followed exactly as described.

Even though extreme care has been taken during the preparation of this manual, neither the publisher nor the author can accept responsibility for any errors in, or omissions from, the information given.

1

Prepare to ride!

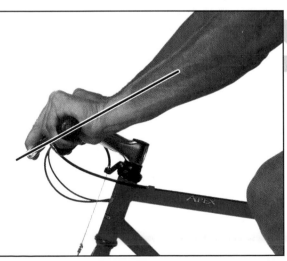

Seat position

Frame size

Handlebar position

Pedals

Mountain bike

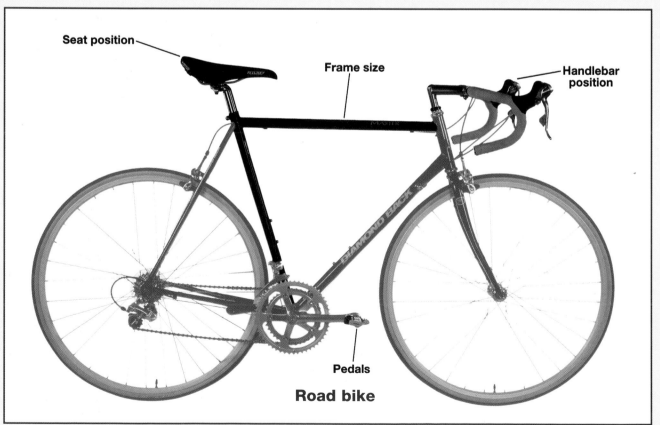

Seat position

Frame size

Handlebar position

Pedals

Road bike

Prepare to ride!

Introduction

Adjusting your bike to fit your body is an important but often overlooked part of the cycling experience. An ill-fitting bike is not only uncomfortable to ride, it's unhealthy. Many physiological problems can be caused or exaggerated by simply not taking the time to get the body-to-bike relationship set up properly. It can also be dangerous. If you don't take the time to position your controls so they are in the most effective, easy-to-operate position, your chances of winding up on the ground or running into something are far greater than if you set up the bike to serve as "an extension of your body."

Invest a little while, and a few dollars if necessary, to custom tune your bike to achieve maximum comfort and efficiency. This will help ensure your cycling career is a long, enjoyable one - even if your rides consist of nothing more than a daily spin around the block.

Contents

1 Frame size

The frame is the cornerstone on which the rest of the bike is built, and is one dimension that hopefully is correct already. If you purchased your bike from a reputable shop or somebody else who knows how a bike should fit, it will be. We'll cover it anyway, because, if for some reason your frame isn't the correct size for you, the rest of this chapter will be a waste of your time.

Swing your leg over the bike and straddle the top tube, with both feet flat on the ground. It is absolutely critical to have some space between the top tube and your crotch (for obvious reasons). But how much? Well, if you have a mountain bike or a hybrid (or are contemplating buying one) there should be two to four inches of clearance. On road bikes there should be a one or two inch gap. **Photo 1**

Not heeding this advice is just asking for injury. Parents, don't buy a bike for your child to "grow into." Kids ride aggressively most of the time and, coupled with the lack of honed riding skills, their feet are going to slip off the pedals occasionally. When this happens they're going to need all the clearance they can get. It's much wiser to spend less money on a bike and get one that fits properly, even if you do have to replace it in a year or two.

1 Frame size
(continued)

The current thinking on fitting a bike is to opt for a frame a little on the small side. Smaller frames weigh less and are stiffer, which makes them more responsive and nimble. This is especially true for mountain bikes, where a quick-handling bike is a real benefit. One thing you'll have to keep in mind, however, is the top tube length. Some frame builders don't construct frames for riders desiring a lower standover height but who still want a normal reach out to the handlebars. Sure, you can install a longer stem to adjust the reach, but a frame that's too short will also give you a wheelbase that is too short, resulting in handling peculiarities when combined with a long stem.

Many women are faced with the problem of top tubes that are too long. Women, on the average, have longer legs and shorter torsos and arms than a man of the same height. When a woman finds a frame that has the proper standover height, it isn't uncommon for her to realize that the reach out to the handlebars is way too far, with her elbows locked straight and her spine nearing horizontal. In this predicament it's far better to go with a smaller frame size, letting the top tube length be the determining factor. You can always raise the seat to compensate.

2 Seat position

This very important adjustment is broken down three ways: Height, tilt, and fore/aft position. You'll know when your seat isn't adjusted properly by the pain it causes - usually where you sit! It can cause knee, ankle, elbow, wrist, back and prostate problems, too.

For the actual adjustment procedures refer to Chapter 10.

2a Seat height

When the seat is set to the proper height you'll get the maximum power from your legs and minimize stress injury to your knees. If your seat is too low, you could develop knee problems. If your hips rock from side-to-side as you pedal, your seat is too high. This causes wasted effort and places too much pressure on your crotch.

To check seat height, sit on the seat and, with your foot on the pedal in the six o'clock position, your leg should be slightly bent - not fully extended. **Photo 2** To verify proper ex-

Note:

If you ride with cycling shoes - cleated or clipless - there should be a 3/16 to 5/16-inch clearance between your heel and the pedal.

tension, place your heel on the pedal. Now your leg should be fully extended, with your heel just touching the pedal (a slight gap is acceptable as long as it doesn't cause your leg to extend fully when you repeat the first check). **Photo 3**

To dial this in, loosen the seat post clamp, move the seat up or down as necessary, then tighten the clamp. Recheck your adjustment.

If you ride a mountain bike you know there are times when a properly adjusted seat simply gets in the way. When riding on rough terrain or on steep descents, ignore the advice given in the previous paragraph and lower your seat to the point that gives you the most confidence and control. In these kind of situations you'll be spending most of your time out of the saddle anyway.

2b Seat tilt

This adjustment is largely a matter of personal preference, but a grossly misadjusted seat can wreak havoc on your body. The best thing to do is to start out with a level seat and ride the bike a few miles. If you feel too much pressure on your undercarriage, lower the nose of the seat a little bit. If you feel like you're sliding toward the front of the bike as you ride, raise the nose a little. Be careful though - a seat that tilts nose-down too far can cause elbow and wrist problems (it shifts too much weight onto your arms), and one that tilts up too radically can irritate a man's prostate. The good news is that this angle, if off by too much, will cause so much discomfort that you aren't likely to ride very far before you fix it! **Photo 4**

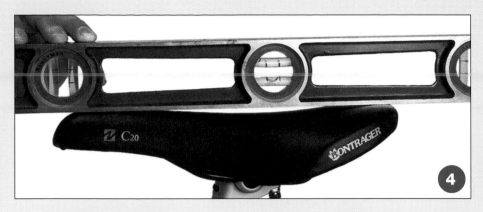

2c Fore/aft position

By loosening the seat clamp bolt you can slide the seat on its rails to the front or rear. To check the position of your seat, sit on the bike and put your feet on the pedals with the crank arms level (do this next to a wall so you don't fall over). Using a plumbline, see where the underside of your kneecap (approximately one-inch in from the outside of your kneecap) is in relation to the centerline of the pedal spindle. It should be directly above it for most riding, but if you typically ride with a high cadence rate (high rpm spinning) move your seat forward about 3/8-inch. Conversely, if you spend a lot of time climbing hills, move the seat to

the rear 3/8 to 9/16-inch for maximum power output. **Photo 5**

3 Handlebar position

This is another adjustment that affects not only your comfort, but your ability to control your bike. For the actual adjustment procedures, refer to Chapter 11.

3a Handlebar height

You'll probably have to do a little experimenting before you settle on the right handlebar height for you and your bike. This setting can range anywhere from two or three inches below the top of the seat to two or three inches above it. Generally, your back should be at approximately a 45-degree angle when riding, slightly less if you ride a road bike (hands on the tops of the bars - not on the lower grips). **Photo 6** With your hands on the drops, your back should be somewhere between 15-degrees to parallel with the ground. **Photo 7** Whatever you ride, your weight should be evenly distributed between your hands and your rear.

Adjustment is carried out by raising or lowering the stem, with the exception of bikes with threadless steerer tubes (Aheadsets) - the only way to adjust these is with an angled stem. The important thing to remember is to not raise the stem up past the minimum insertion point marked on the stem. If you find that when the stem is raised to that point but the handlebars are still too low for you, a stem with a greater rise or raised handlebars will have to be considered.

3b Reach

If you find that the reach out to the handlebars is too far (locking your elbows straight) or too short (which will cause you to feel "cramped" on the bike and may even result in your knees hitting the handlebars) you can remedy this problem by changing stems. Stems are available in a wide

variety of lengths and rises, so there's bound to be one that suits your needs. Keep this in mind: Stem length directly affects steering characteristics and front-to-rear weight distribution. Installing a longer stem will "slow down" your steering, making your bike a bit less responsive. On the other hand, installing a shorter stem will have the opposite affect.

3b.1 Road bikes

To determine the proper reach on a road bike, sit on the bike and assume your normal riding position. Now look down over the front of the handlebars - your view of the front axle should just be obscured. If the reach is too short and you find that a stem longer than 4-1/2 inches is required, the top tube of your frame is too short. **Photo 8**

3b.2 Mountain bikes and hybrids

Determining reach on one of these bikes is really a matter of personal preference. If you ride hard and aggressively most of the time, a longer stem will probably make you happiest. **Photo 9** If sightseeing and slower paced riding is your cup of tea, you may be more comfortable with a slightly shorter stem that will allow you to sit in a more upright position. Just make sure your knees don't hit the ends of the handlebars while making shallow turns. **Photo 10**

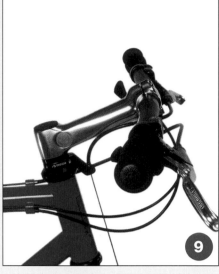

3c Tilt
3c.1 Road bikes

The typical drop bars found on most road bikes have an acceptable range of rotation in which they can be positioned. Anything outside of this range will not only create a dangerous condition, it'll look stupid.

The highest allowable position of the bar results in the part of the bar pointing forward being level with the part that goes through the stem. If your rides aren't too spirited and you rest your hands on the brake hoods most of the time you might find this comfortable. **Photo 11**

The lowest allowable rotation is achieved when the lower part of the grip is level, or parallel with the ground. If you like to ride fast and spend much

of your time in a tuck, you'll probably opt for this setting. **Photo 12**

As with many things, compromise may be the best bet. A bar placed midway between these two extremes offers some of the advantages of both.

3c.2 Mountain bikes and hybrids

Although they sometimes appear straight, mountain bike bars are available in a variety of bends. Bars with a very shallow bend (3-degrees or so) tend to force your elbows out away from your body and are designed for aggressive riding. Bars with a little more bend in them may be more comfortable, as your hand will grip them more naturally. In any case, the profile of either type can be adjusted by loosening the stem clamp and rotating the

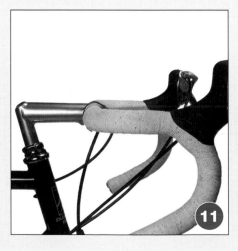

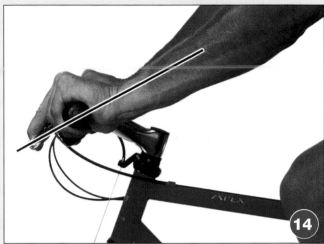

bar to obtain the most natural positioning of your wrist. Be careful though - rotating the bars down too far could cause your hands to slip off the grips.

3d Brake/shift lever position

Whatever handlebar position you decide on, make sure you check your ability to operate the brake levers and, on mountain bikes and hybrids, the shift levers. If you determine that your brake levers are in need of repositioning, refer to Chapter 9 for the adjustment procedure. If the shifters aren't where they should be, follow the adjustment procedure given in Chapter 7.

3d.1 Road bikes

You should be able to effectively squeeze the levers while your hands are resting on the brake hoods, bringing the bike to a quick stop. If the levers are located too far down on the drops, this might not be possible. **Photo 13**

You should also be able to grasp the levers while your hands are in the center portion of the drop without having to angle your hands in an upward direction. If you have to do this, the levers are positioned too high.

3d.2 Mountain bikes and hybrids

Sit on the bike and hold onto the handlebars as you normally would when you ride. The angle of the brake levers should generally be in line with your forearms. You shouldn't have to twist your wrist in either direction for your fingers to grasp the brake levers. If you do, adjust the levers up or down, as necessary, to make them easiest to grab. See Chapter 9 for the brake lever adjusting procedure. **Photo 14**

Also, the levers should be easy to pull with just your index and middle fingers - they should make contact right at the part of the lever nearest the handlebar. If they aren't in the right spot, move them inward or outward as required.

The shift levers should be easy to operate, without having to reposition your hands on the grips to upshift or downshift.

Helmets and gloves

Don't forget to wear an approved helmet when you ride. Even though you may take the time to get your bike properly set up, there's no guarantee that you won't come off it! If that happens, chances are you won't land on your feet.

Gloves are also highly recommended. Even the half-finger style offers adequate protection, as most abrasion injuries to the hands involve the palms. A good pair of gloves will also reduce road shock felt through the handlebars and eliminate slippery grips caused by sweat.

4 Pedals

4a Clipless type pedals

Most clipless type pedals allow for a little play (in and out movement of the heel), but you should make sure that your cleat is centered in the pedal according to your foot alignment. This way your heels will be less likely to contact the chainstays or accidentally release from the pedal.

The easiest way to do this is to get on your bike, click your shoes into the pedals (do this next to an immovable object that you can hold on to) and position the crank arms in the nine and three o'clock positions. Relax and allow your feet to find the most comfortable pedaling position, then note their relationship to the crank arm and chain stay. Now, untie (or un-Velcro) your shoes and take your feet out, leaving the shoes attached to the pedals. Move the heel of each shoe in and out, feeling for the limit of rotation. When the cleats are adjusted properly, the shoes should be able to rotate in and out to an equal degree before resistance from the pedal is encountered. If not, release the shoe from the pedal, loosen the cleat and reposition it as necessary. **Photo 15**

The cleat should be positioned so the ball of your foot is directly over the pedal when you click in. If it isn't, adjust the cleat forward or backward on the shoe so it will be.

Lastly, be sure to set the pedal tension, if it's adjustable. You should have no trouble releasing your foot from the pedal by moving your heel in an outward direction. If it takes more than just a little effort to twist your feet out, loosen the pedal tension. As you gain confidence in your ability to detach your feet when you need to, you can increase the tension. **Photo 16**

4b Slotted type cleats

This kind of shoe doesn't allow any rotational play of the foot, so it is very important to position the cleat on the shoe to provide the natural rotation of your foot as you pedal. To do this, slightly loosen the cleat mounting screws, then get on your bike and ride it. Your foot should move the cleat to the position that is the most natural for you. When you have found that position, loosen the straps and carefully detach your feet from the pedals, without disturbing the cleats. Tighten the cleat mounting screws securely. **Photo 17**

And, just like any pedal, the ball of your foot should be positioned over the center of the pedal. Move the cleat up or back on the shoe to achieve this.

4c Mountain bike/hybrid pedals with toe clips and straps

Loosen the toe clip straps and place your foot on the pedal. The ball

of your foot should be centered over the pedal spindle, and there shouldn't be too much space between the toe of your shoe and the end of the toe clip.

Toe clips generally come in three sizes: small, medium and large. If you find that the toe clip prevents your foot from resting on the pedal properly, try the next size up. If there's too much space between your toe and the toe clip when your foot is positioned properly, change to a smaller size.

Routine maintenance

Maintenance schedule

An interesting phenomenon occurs when you ignore your bike's need for routine care. It wears out! It may seem fine as you ride it month after neglected month. That's because the degradation is so insidious that you won't notice anything wrong until a component fails or you remove a wheel to repair a flat and discover that you can't turn the axle by hand. Or maybe you loaned your bike to a friend, only to have him bring it back shaking his head and wearing a disgusted look. It's kind of like that "frog in the hot water" experiment.

If you religiously perform your pre-ride checks and keep your bike clean and lubricated, your bike will ride better, look sharper and last longer. Periodically, however, you'll have to go a little deeper into the realm of cycle maintenance to clean, lubricate and adjust the things you can't get to externally.

Daily, or before each ride

- Perform the *Pre-ride checks* as described earlier in this Chapter

After each ride

- Clean your bike (if necessary)
- Lubricate all pivot points
- Lubricate the chain

Monthly

- Clean the brake pads and the braking surfaces on the rims with rubbing alcohol
- Check the tightness of the crank bolts or nuts with a wrench (not just by wiggling the crank arms (see Chapter 5)
- Clean and inspect the chain - lubricate or replace it as necessary (see Chapter 8)
- Inspect the condition of the chainrings and the sprockets for excessive wear (see Chapter 8). Repair or replace parts as required.
- Check the condition of the toe straps and clips. If the straps are leather, apply leather preservative.

Every six months

All items listed above, plus:

- Disassemble, clean, inspect and repack the hub bearings (see Chapter 4)
- Check spoke tension, tighten and true-up wheel as necessary (see Chapter 4)
- Disassemble, clean, inspect and repack the bottom bracket bearings (non-cartridge type) (see Chapter 5)
- Disassemble, clean, inspect and repack the pedal bearings (see Chapter 5)
- Inspect, clean and thoroughly lubricate all control cables (see Chapter 6).
- Remove and clean the rear derailleur guide and tension wheels, thoroughly clean the derailleur (see Chapter 7)
- Remove the seatpost from the frame, clean and lubricate it (see Chapter 10)
- Remove the stem from the steerer tube, clean and lubricate it (see Chapter 11)
- Disassemble, clean, inspect and repack the headset bearings (see Chapter 11)

2 Routine maintenance

Introduction

This chapter will establish the key to the longevity of your bike. If followed, your bike will be much more pleasurable to ride. It will also help you find potential problems before they grow into major ones, which will make your cycling experience much safer.

The chapter is divided into two parts: Pre-ride inspection and post-ride cleaning and lubrication. A routine maintenance schedule is included on the opposite page.

Contents

1 Pre-ride inspection

The following quick-checks should be made before every ride. The first three areas - brakes, tires and wheels - **must** be checked before you get on your bike. The remaining areas should be looked at to prevent an untimely breakdown or unpleasant riding. Try to get in the habit of performing these checks the night before a ride. That way, you won't be sidelined if you notice a broken component, or your friends won't have to wait for you as you fix a flat tire, adjust your brakes and derailleur, lubricate your chain, etc.

If you don't normally check over your bike before you set off for a ride, the following information will probably seem like overkill. Once you become familiar with the checking procedures, however, you'll find that they really don't take much time at all. And if you've ever spent time in the hospital because your front wheel fell off, or have been stranded fifteen miles from home because your chain tore out most of the spokes on your back wheel, you'll understand that these checks, in the long run, will actually save you time and money.

The procedures here are limited to checks of the various systems on your bike. The actual adjustment or repair procedures are located in their appropriate chapters.

Brakes

See Chapter 9 for brake adjustments and repairs

Open the brake quick release or detach the link wire and check the condition and thickness of the brake pads. They should have plenty of rubber left, and the composition of the rubber shouldn't be rock-hard (you should be able to scratch it with your fingernail). Also check for imbedded foreign matter. If the friction material is deteriorated, hardened or too thin, replace the pads.

Make sure there is adequate clearance between the pad and the innermost circumference of the braking surface. If the pads ride too low on the rim, like the one shown in this photo, they could slip off the rim during heavy braking, causing a loss of braking and tearing out spokes (with disastrous results).

Reconnect the link wire or, on side-pull brakes, make sure the quick-release is *closed completely*.

Check the position of the brake pad to the rim. It shouldn't be any closer than 1 mm (about 3/64-inch) to the edge of the rim - if it is, the tire could be damaged by the pad rubbing against it. Check the tightness of the brake pad nuts and other brake attaching fasteners.

Check the freeplay of the brake levers. The levers should actuate the brakes near the beginning of their travel, but there should be about 3/4 to 1-1/2 inches of play before engagement is felt. The levers should also be tight on the handlebars.

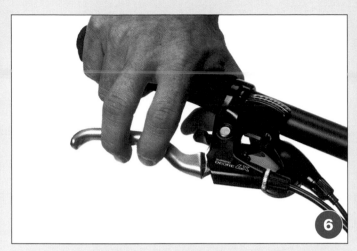

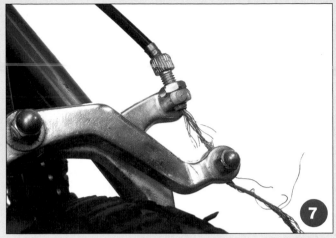

More importantly, there should be plenty of room between the brake levers and the handlebar when you squeeze the brake levers hard. If you tend to pull the levers with your index and middle fingers, make sure the levers don't contact the knuckles on your remaining fingers. If there isn't adequate clearance, adjust the brakes.

Check the condition of the brake cables along their entire length. If they're dry or slightly rusty, lubricate them (see Chapter 6). If they're cut or frayed, replace them (also see Chapter 6).

Tires

Wheels

See Chapter 4 for wheel and hub servicing procedures

Check the tire pressure using an accurate gauge, comparing your reading with the recommended inflation pressure molded into the sidewall of the tire. Add air if they're low.

Check the tires for cracks, bulges and bald spots. Replace them if necessary (see Chapter 4).

Shake each wheel from side-to-side, checking for loose hub bearings. If they're loose, adjust them so all play is taken out.

1 Pre-ride inspection (continued)

Wheels (continued)

A wheel with loose spokes isn't a very strong wheel. Check the tension of the spokes by squeezing paired spokes together. If they're loose, tighten them a bit and attempt to true-up the wheel (be very careful - it's easy to completely mess-up a wheel with a spoke wrench!). Also, check for bent or broken spokes.

Spin each wheel and check for trueness by looking at the gaps between the rim and the brake pads. If the brakes are adjusted properly but the rim contacts either brake pad at any point in its rotation, the rim should be trued. Ideally, there should be no lateral movement of the rim. Also, check that the radius of the wheel doesn't change as the wheel rotates. Rims that don't run true waste energy, will cause a surging sensation while braking, and are prone to collapse during vigorous (especially off-road) riding.

Check the rims for bulges and dings. Damage like this can cause loose spokes and pulsating brakes. Also check for splits at the seam where an extruded rim has been joined.

If your bike is equipped with quick-release hubs, make sure the levers are tightly secured. The quick-releases on later model bikes are marked OPEN and CLOSE - make sure the CLOSE marking is visible. They should be set tight enough that the lever leaves an imprint on your hand after closing it. If the lever closes too easy, open it back up, tighten the nut on the other side, then close the lever again. Repeat this until the force required to close the lever is adequate.

If your bike has regular axle nuts, check their tightness with a wrench.

Headset bearings

Straddle the bike, firmly squeeze the front brake lever and push and pull on the handlebars. If the headset bearings are loose, you'll feel a definite clunking. Tighten the headset if necessary (see Chapter 11).

Note:

A loose headset can lead to severe wobble at higher speeds, which can cause you to crash. It can also cause rapid disintegration of the headset bearings.

Stem, handlebar and (if equipped) bar end tightness

See Chapter 11 for procedures related to the stem and handlebars

Straddle the front wheel, grasp the handlebars and attempt to twist them back and forth. If the stem moves in the steerer tube (or on it, if your bike has a threadless, or Aheadset, type of headset) it must be tightened (see Chapter 11). Also, check the stem for cracks. DO NOT ride with a cracked stem!

Now, attempt to twist the handlebars in the stem. They shouldn't budge. Tighten the clamp bolt on the stem if necessary.

If the handlebar is equipped with bar ends, make sure you can't twist them on the handlebar.

See Chapter 7 for the derailleur adjustment procedure

Support the bike in a workstand or have a friend hold the bike with the rear wheel off the ground. Turn the cranks and shift the rear derailleur through the gears. Make sure the derailleur travel limit screws are properly set - the chain shouldn't jump off the largest or the smallest sprocket. If it does, it could tear out spokes or get jammed between the frame and the sprocket.

Repeat this check on the front chainrings.

Chain

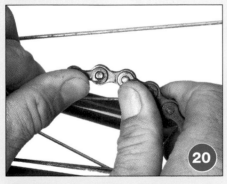

Check the entire length of the chain for stiff or frozen links. If you find any, lubricate the stiff link with WD40 or chain lubricant, then work the link free by flexing it from side-to-side and bending it in its normal plane until it is loose.

Derailleur adjustment

Crank arms and bottom bracket bearings

Grab each crank arm and try to shake it in and out. If you feel any play, check the tightness of the crank arm bolts or nuts. If they're tight, your bottom bracket is in need of adjustment (if possible), repair or replacement. See Chapter 5 for crankset and bottom bracket service procedures.

Check the tightness of the chainring bolts with an Allen wrench.

Pedals

Turn each pedal on its spindle, making sure it moves freely without binding or roughness. Pull the pedal away from the crank - there should be no freeplay in this direction. Service the pedals as soon as possible if they don't pass (see Chapter 5).

Seat and seat post

Grasp the seat, attempting to tilt it up and down. If the seat moves, tighten the seat clamp. Also try to twist the seat side-to-side. If it moves, tighten the seat clamp or the seat post clamp, as necessary (See Chapter 10).

Frame

Carefully check the frame for cracks, especially in the area where the top tube and down tube meet the head tube. If you find any cracks, DON'T ride the bike! Buy a new frame or consult a frame repair specialist to see if the damage can be fixed.

2 Post-ride cleaning and lubrication

A bicycle's worst enemy is dirt, followed closely by water (which helps the dirt find its way into all of the places you don't want it). Once dirt finds its way into shifting mechanisms and bearings it acts as an abrasive, gradually destroying bearing surfaces and wearing out other components. It doesn't do your bike's finish any good, either.

Unfortunately, the only way to really get your bike clean is to use water, soap and, when necessary, degreaser. Through careful use of these three ingredients you can slow down the damage process that dirt will inevitably cause.

Wash your bike as often as necessary. If you ride in wet weather or muddy conditions you should wash your bike after every ride - especially if you live in areas where the roads are salted. As for mud, don't give it a

chance to dry - wash it off as soon as possible. Keep in mind that after extremely wet, muddy rides you should disassemble your hubs, clean the bearings and repack them with grease. This will lengthen their lifespan and keep rolling resistance to a minimum.

You don't need any fancy equipment to wash your bike effectively. A bucket of soapy water (dishwashing soap works fine), a spray bottle filled with a mild degreaser, a rag or sponge, a stiff (but soft-bristled) brush and a hose. For best results, a chain cleaning tool and sprocket scraper can be used, and make a lot of sense because the chain and sprockets are the hardest parts of a bike to get clean.

Cleaning

Begin by washing down the bike with water from a hose. A high-pressure nozzle is not recommended - just let the water flow from the hose and onto the bike. Don't point the hose directly at the hub or bottom bracket bearings. If the bike is muddy, try to get all the mud off at this stage.

Use the brush on hard-to-get-at areas like around the brakes, hub flanges, shift levers, knobby tires, etc.

If the sprockets are caked with grime, scrape and brush off as much of it as possible. A narrow-bladed screwdriver can be used, but the Gearclean Brush by Park Tool greatly simplifies this process. Also, get as much of this stuff off of the chain as you can.

Spray a mild degreasing solution onto the freewheel assembly. After letting it "work" for a few minutes, take the brush to the sprockets.

Don't forget the guide and tension wheels of the derailleur . . .

. . . or the teeth of the chainrings . . .

. . . or the chain. If the chain is extremely dirty, clean it as described in Chapter 8.

Rinse off the sprockets, derailleurs, chainrings and chain with water. Sometimes it takes more than one application of degreaser and some vigorous brushing to get the sprockets clean.

Now, take the rag or sponge, plunge it into the bucket of soapy water and wipe down the entire bike.

Hose down the bike once again, making sure all of the soap is rinsed off.

Bounce the bike on its tires to get most of the water off. If you're concerned about water spots, wipe down the frame with a soft cloth.

Lubrication

38

Spray WD40 or an equivalent penetrating lubricant into all of the moving parts of the bike, such as the brake pivots (be careful not to get any on the pads or rim) . . .

39

. . . the derailleur pivots (the front derailleur, too) . . .

40

. . . the derailleur tension and guide wheels . . .

41

. . . the brake lever pivots . . .

42

. . . the control cables, where they enter their casings . . .

That's it! But wait - if you're not a procrastinator, go ahead and perform the pre-ride checks described previously. That way, you'll just have to check the tire pressures the next time you want to hop on your bike!

43

. . . and the chain. It's a good idea to lube the chain with a heavier chain lubricant afterwards, but the WD40 will displace all the water. Be careful not to get any on the rim and be sure to wipe off the excess.

Troubleshooting

Wear and component failure is normal for any mechanical device. If you perform your pre-ride checks as described in Chapter 2, rectify problems as soon as you notice them and keep your bike clean and well lubricated, you'll slow down the wear process and prolong the life of your bike's components. Hopefully, you won't need to use this chapter very often.

Even when a bicycle is properly maintained, problems can still occur. This is especially true with mountain bikes, as they take quite a bit more punishment than bikes that are used primarily on the road.

Some problems are easy to diagnose and fix, while others aren't so obvious. There is nothing "mysterious" about troubleshooting a bicycle, however - you don't have to be a professional mechanic. Successful troubleshooting is simply the result of a bit of knowledge combined with an intelligent, systematic approach to the problem. Always work by process of elimination when tackling a problem that isn't readily diagnosed, starting with the simplest solution and working through to the most complex.

This chapter provides an easy reference guide to the more common problems that may crop up during normal operation of your bicycle. In the following table, problems will be listed under the system or component group that they pertain to. The first group encompasses general riding problems that aren't easily categorized. The bold headings contain the various problems that may be encountered. The left column lists the probable cause(s) of the problem, and the right column reveals the corrective action necessary to restore proper operation.

If, after using this troubleshooting guide you are still unable to resolve the problem, don't be afraid to seek the advice of your local bike shop. They're in business because they love bicycles, and will be more than happy to help you.

General riding problems

(Refer to this section in case you aren't sure where to start)

Bike feels shaky or wobbly

Loose hub bearings . . . . Adjust the hub bearings (see Chapter 4)

Loose headset bearings . . . . Adjust the headset (see Chapter 11)

Bike is hard to pedal (but coasts okay)

Bottom bracket bearings misadjusted, ... Disassemble, clean and inspect the bottom bracket (non-cartridge
worn or in need of service   type), lubricate or replace as necessary (see Chapter 5).

Chain worn or in need of service . . . . Service or replace the chain as necessary (see Chapter 8)

General riding problems (continued)

Bike doesn't coast well

Brakes rubbing on rim . . . . Adjust the brakes (see Chapter 9)

Hub bearings worn or in need of service . . . . . . Disassemble, inspect and clean the hub bearings, lubricate or replace as necessary (see Chapter 4)

Clicking, popping, squeaking or creaking noises while pedaling only

Pedal(s) loose on crank arm(s) . . . . Tighten the pedal(s) (see Chapter 5)

Pedal bearings dry or worn . . . . Disassemble pedal (if possible), inspect pedal bearings, lubricate or replace as necessary (see Chapter 5)

Pedal cage loose on pedal . . . . Tighten pedal cage screws (see Chapter 5)

Loose toe clip fasteners . . . . Tighten toe clip fasteners

Loose chainring bolts . . . . Tighten chainring bolts (see Chapter 5)

Loose crank arm(s) . . . . Tighten crank arm bolt(s) or nut(s) (see Chapter 5). If it's still loose, the crank arm(s) may be worn out.

Spot weld on chainring broken . . . . Replace crankset (see Chapter 5)
    (non-removable chainrings)

Bottom bracket bearings worn, dry or . . . . Disassemble, clean and inspect bottom bracket, lubricate and adjust or
    out of adjustment (non-cartridge type)   replace as required (see Chapter 5)

Bottom bracket loose in frame or worn . . . . Tighten or replace bottom bracket as necessary
    (cartridge type)

Loose handlebar binder bolt (pedaling . . . . Tighten binder bolt
    under heavy load, pulling on bars)

Stem bolt loose (pedaling under heavy load, . . . Tighten stem bolt
    pulling on bars)

Stem rusty or dry in steerer tube (pedaling . . . . Remove stem, clean and lubricate (See Chapter 11)
    under heavy load, pulling on bars)

Frame cracked . . . . Inspect frame thoroughly, repair or replace frame

Chain dry or dirty . . . . Clean and lubricate chain (see Chapter 8)

Chain worn out . . . . Replace chain (and inspect sprockets and chainrings, replacing parts as necessary (see Chapters 5 and 8)

Chainring(s) worn or bent/dented . . . . Straighten bent chainring teeth if possible, or replace chainring(s) (see Chapter 5)

Popping or clicking sounds while pedaling or coasting

Loose spokes . . . . Tighten spokes and true-up wheel (see Chapter 4)

Bike pulls to one side (especially when you let go of the handlebars)

Frame bent . . . . Have frame straightened or replace frame

Forks bent . . . . Replace forks (see Chapter 11)

Wheels, hubs and tires

Tires go flat repeatedly

Valve stem core loose . . . . Tighten valve stem core (see Chapter 4)

Tires worn too thin . . . . Replace tires (see Chapter 4)

Thorn stuck in tire . . . . Remove tire, carefully check inside of tire for thorn (see Chapter 4)

Rim tape or strip missing or mispositioned, ... Remove tire and tube, install or reposition rim tape or strip (see Chapter 4)
    allowing spoke nipples to contact tube

End of spoke protruding past nipple and . . . . . . Install shorter spoke or file off excess from spoke end
    contacting tube

Air pressure in tire too low . . . . Inflate tires to proper pressure

Too many hazards in your riding area . . . . Install "Slime" or equivalent tube sealer in tubes

Wheel doesn't spin well or axles hard to turn (with wheel removed)

Hub bearings too tight . . . . Adjust hub bearings (see Chapter 4)

Hub bearings in need of service . . . . Disassemble hub, clean and inspect hub and bearings, lubricate or
    replace as required (see Chapter 4)

Wheel or axle feels "notchy" when turned slowly by hand

Hub bearings in need of service . . . . Disassemble hub, clean and inspect hub and bearings, lubricate or replace
    as required (see Chapter 4)

Hub bearings, hub and/or cones worn . . . . Disassemble, clean and inspect hub and bearing components, lubricate or
    (most likely) replace hubs (see Chapter 4)

Crankset and pedals

Noises while pedaling

See items under *General riding problems* heading

Chainrings worn

Normal wear . . . . Replace chainring(s) (see Chapter 5)

Worn-out chain . . . . Replace chain and chainrings (see Chapters 5 and 8)

Chainring rubs against front derailleur

Front derailleur out of adjustment . . . . Adjust front derailleur (see Chapter 7)

Chainring bent . . . . Straighten or replace chainring (see Chapter 5)

Crank arm spider bent . . . . Replace crank arm (see Chapter 5)

Crankset and pedals (continued)

Cranks hard to turn or are noisy

Bottom bracket bearings in need of service . . . .   Disassemble, clean and inspect bottom bracket, replacing or relubing as required
    or are worn out   (non-cartridge type) or replace bottom bracket (cartridge type) (see Chapter 5)

Pedal wobbles on spindle

Loose or worn pedal bearings . . . .   Adjust pedal bearings, if possible, or replace pedals (see Chapter 5)

Pedals don't turn freely on spindle

Pedal bearings too tight . . . .   Adjust pedal bearings, if possible, or replace pedals
    (see Chapter 5)

Pedal bearings in need of service . . . .   Disassemble, clean and inspect pedal bearings (if possible), lubricate and
    reassemble pedals (see Chapter 5)

Shifters and derailleurs

Hard to shift gears (front or rear)

Shift cable dry or worn . . . .   Lubricate or replace shift cable (see Chapter 6)

Derailleur dirty or worn . . . .   Clean or replace derailleur (see Chapter 7)

Derailleur slips out of gear (front or rear)

Index shifters - shifter detents worn out . . . .   Replace shifter (see Chapter 7)

Non-index shifters - shifter tension . . . .   Tighten tension screw or replace friction washers (see Chapter 7)
    screw loose or friction washers worn out

Delayed shifts (front or rear)

Shift cable dry, rusty or worn . . . .   Clean and lubricate or replace cable (see Chapter 6)

Derailleur sticky or worn . . . .   Clean and lubricate or replace derailleur (see Chapter 7)

Chain "clatters" on sprockets

Rear derailleur shift indexing out of adjustment .   Adjust rear derailleur shift cable (see Chapter 7)

Rear derailleur guide pulley worn out . . . .   Replace guide pulley (see Chapter 7)

Chain falls off sprockets while shifting

Rear derailleur stop screws out of adjustment . .   If the chain falls off into the spokes, adjust the "L" stop screw. If the chain
    falls off between sprocket and frame, adjust the "H" stop screw (see Chapter 7).

Rear derailleur won't shift chain to biggest sprocket (lowest gear)

Rear derailleur stop screw misadjusted . . . .   Adjust "L" stop screw on rear derailleur (see Chapter 7)

Rear derailleur shift cable out of adjustment, . . .   Adjust, lubricate or replace rear derailleur shift cable (see Chapter 6)
    sticky or worn

Rear derailleur won't shift chain to smallest sprocket (highest gear)

Rear derailleur stop screw misadjusted . . . . Adjust "H" stop screw on rear derailleur (see Chapter 7)

Rear derailleur shift cable out of adjustment, . . . Adjust, lubricate or replace rear derailleur shift cable (see Chapter 6)
    sticky or worn

Rear derailleur return spring weak . . . . Replace return spring or rear derailleur (see Chapter 7)

Rear derailleur extremely dirty . . . . Clean and lubricate rear derailleur (see Chapter 2)

Rear derailleur does not shift accurately

Rear derailleur indexing out of adjustment . . . . . Adjust rear derailleur shift cable (see Chapter 7)

Rear derailleur shift cable sticky or worn . . . . . . Lubricate or replace rear derailleur shift cable (see Chapter 6)

Rear derailleur worn out . . . . Replace rear derailleur (see Chapter 7)

Front derailleur won't shift chain to biggest chainring

Front derailleur stop screw misadjusted . . . . Adjust outer (H) stop screw (see Chapter 7)

Front derailleur shift cable out of . . . . Adjust, lubricate or replace front derailleur shift cable (see Chapter 6)
    adjustment or sticky

Front derailleur won't shift chain to smallest chainring

Front derailleur stop screw misadjusted . . . . Adjust inner (L) stop screw (see Chapter 7)

Front derailleur shift cable out of adjustment, . . . Adjust, lubricate or replace front derailleur shift cable (see Chapter 6)
    worn or sticky

Front derailleur return spring weak . . . . Replace spring or front derailleur (see Chapter 7)

Front derailleur extremely dirty . . . . Clean and lubricate the front derailleur (see Chapter 2)

Front derailleur cage bent or spread open . . . . . Straighten cage or replace derailleur (see Chapter 7)

Front derailleur shifting not precise or is inconsistent

Front derailleur not positioned properly . . . . Move derailleur down into proper position, or adjust until derailleur
    cage plates are parallel with the chainrings (see Chapter 7)

Derailleur inner plate excessively worn . . . . Replace derailleur (see Chapter 7)

Front derailleur shift cable sticky or worn . . . . . . Lubricate or replace cable (see Chapter 6)

Front derailleur rubs on chain in more than one chainring

Front derailleur crooked . . . . Adjust front derailleur parallel with chainrings (see Chapter 7)

Chainrings bent . . . . Straighten or replace chainrings (see Chapter 5)

Crank arm spider bent . . . . Replace crank arm (see Chapter 5)

Front derailleur rubs on chain in middle or big chainring

Shifter indexing out of adjustment . . . . Adjust front derailleur shift cable tension (see Chapter 7)

Chain and sprockets

Chain is noisy (squeaky or "crunchy")

Dirty chain . . . . Clean and lubricate chain (see Chapter 8)

Chain worn out . . . . Replace chain (see Chapter 8). Also, inspect chainrings and sprockets, replacing parts as necessary (see Chapters 5 and 8)

Chain "skips" or clicks loudly in the same spot, every revolution of the chain

The chain has a stiff link . . . . Free-up the stiff link (see Chapters 2 and 8), lubricate the chain regularly (see Chapter 2)

Chain "skips" while pedaling

Worn chain . . . . Replace chain (see Chapter 8)

Worn sprockets . . . . Replace sprockets and chain (see Chapter 8)

Note: *Whenever replacing sprockets, install a new chain, too.*

Chain has too much slack (single speed bikes or bikes with hub gears)

Rear wheel not positioned properly . . . . Adjust wheel to the rear until there is only a little slack in the chain

Chain worn out . . . . Replace the chain (see Chapter 8)

Chain falls off the chainrings or sprockets when shifting

See items under *Shifters and derailleurs*

Freewheel makes a lot of noise while coasting

Freewheel dirty or in need of lubrication . . . . Clean and lubricate freewheel or freehub (see Chapter 8)

Freewheel doesn't spin or spins both ways

Freewheel mechanism dirty . . . . Clean and lubricate freewheel or freehub (see Chapter 8)

Freewheel broken . . . . Replace freewheel or freehub (see Chapter 8)

Sprockets worn out

Normal wear . . . . Replace freewheel assembly or freehub sprocket cluster (or individual sprockets) (see Chapter 8). Also replace the chain.

Chain worn out . . . . See above

Troubleshooting

Brakes

Brake pad(s) rub on rim

Brake not centered . . . . Adjust (center) brake (see Chapter 9)

Wheel out of true . . . . True-up wheel (see Chapter 4)

Brake return spring(s) weak . . . . Adjust or replace spring(s) (see Chapter 9)

Brake not returning fully due to sticky operation . Disassemble brake, clean and lubricate pivot points (see Chapter 9)

Brake not returning fully due to sticky cable . . . . Clean and lubricate or replace cable (see Chapter 6)

Brake pads worn unevenly

Brake not adjusted properly . . . . Replace pads and adjust brake (see Chapter 9)

Brake not centered . . . . Adjust (center) brake (see Chapter 9)

Brakes squeal

Rims and pads dirty . . . . Clean rims and pads with rubbing alcohol (rims may have to be cleaned with a *mild* abrasive) (see Chapter 9)

Pads worn or hardened . . . . Replace pads (see Chapter 9)

Wrong type of brake pad compound . . . . Try a different type of pad

Brake pads not toed-in . . . . Adjust pad toe-in (see Chapter 9)

Brake lever(s) hard to pull

Brake cable(s) dry . . . . Lubricate cable(s) (see Chapter 6)

Brake cable(s) and/or casing(s) worn . . . . Replace cable(s) (see Chapter 6)

Brake not properly adjusted . . . . Adjust brakes (see Chapter 9)

Brake arms and supports corroded or dirty . . . . Remove brake arms, clean arms and supports (see Chapter 9)

Brake lever pivot dry . . . . Lubricate lever pivot (see Chapter 2)

Bike surges or shakes when braking

Rim dented . . . . Repair or replace rim (see Chapter 4)

Wheel out of true . . . . True-up wheel (see Chapter 4)

Brake arms loose . . . . Tighten and, if necessary, adjust brakes (see Chapter 9)

Headset loose . . . . Adjust headset (see Chapter 11)

Brakes ineffective

Brakes out of adjustment . . . . Adjust brakes (see Chapter 9)

Brake pads worn or hardened . . . . Replace pads (see Chapter 9)

Rims dirty . . . . Clean rims with rubbing alcohol (and a *mild* abrasive, if necessary) (see Chapter 9)

Brake cable/casing dry, rusty or worn . . . . Inspect cable and casing, lubricate or replace as required (see Chapter 9)

Brake pads rub on tire or drop off rim when applied

Brake out of adjustment . . . . Adjust brake immediately (see Chapter 9)

Seat and seat post

Seat post seized in seat tube

Seat post corroded . . . .   Apply penetrating oil around the post, wait awhile, then try to remove it. If you still can't remove it, take the bike to a bike shop. Be sure to lubricate the post with grease when reinstalling (see Chapter 10).

Seat won't maintain position

Seat clamp loose or worn . . . .   Tighten or replace seat clamp (see Chapter 10)

Seat post loose . . . .   Tighten seat post clamp

Wrong size seat post . . . .   Seat posts are available in many diameters. Be sure your seat post is the correct diameter for your seat tube (consult a bike shop for help).

Steering

Steering feels loose in some positions and tight in others

Bent fork steerer tube . . . .   Replace the steerer tube (if possible, and this is a job for a bike shop) or the entire fork (in this case a bike shop will probably have to cut the steerer tube to the proper length) (see Chapter 11)

Steering fells "notchy"

Headset bearing races damaged . . . .   Replace headset (see Chapter 11)

Too much effort required to turn handlebars

Headset bearings too tight . . . .   Adjust headset (see Chapter 11)

Headset bearings in need of service . . . .   Disassemble, clean and inspect the headset bearings and races. Lubricate or replace as necessary (see Chapter 11)

Front end rattles over bumps

Loose headset . . . .   Adjust headset (see Chapter 11)

Headset keeps loosening up

Threads on steerer tube damaged . . . .   Replace the steerer tube (if possible, and this is a job for a bike shop) or the entire fork (in this case a bike shop will probably have to cut the steerer tube to the proper length) (see Chapter 11)

Headset locknut not tightened securely . . . .   Tighten securely with proper headset wrenches (not pliers!)

Stem seized in steerer tube

Stem corroded . . . .   Apply penetrating oil around the stem, wait awhile, then try to remove it. If you still can't remove it, take the bike to a bike shop. Be sure to lubricate the stem with grease when reinstalling (see Chapter 11).

4

Wheels, tires and hubs

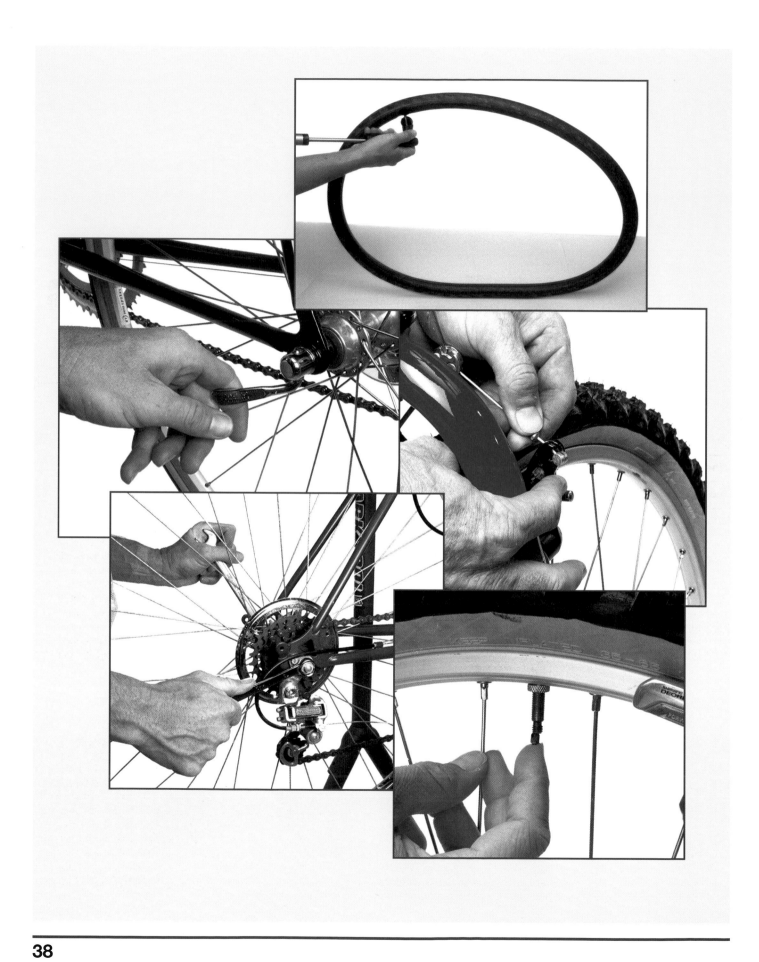

4 Wheels, tires and hubs

Contents

Introduction

This chapter deals with the components of your bike that allow it to roll. These parts include the tires, tubes, rims, spokes, hubs, bearings, axles and axle quick releases.

Keeping these components in good order is necessary for safe, or even tolerable, operation of the bicycle. The wheels, tires and hubs are some of the most abused, neglected and vulnerable pieces of your bike, and an unexpected problem with any one of them can send you on a long walk home, pushing or carrying your bike, if you aren't prepared.

1 Wheel removal and installation

Removal

Removing wheels is probably the most common service procedure you will find yourself doing to your bike.

You have to remove wheels to fix flat tires, change tires, service the hub bearings, replace your rear sprockets or service your freewheel, and sometimes just to get them out of the way to clean your bike when it's really dirty.

First, it's necessary to get the wheel to be removed off the ground. If you're out in the field or on the road you can lay the bike down on it's *left* side (bikes with derailleurs). If you're at home, though, support the bike on a repair stand if you have one, or hang it up with a piece of rope looped over the rafters. If you're careful, you can turn the bike upside down and stand it on the seat and handlebars, as long as you place a couple of two-by-fours under the handlebars so the brake levers and shifters don't get damaged.

If you're removing a rear wheel on a bike with coaster brakes, detach the brake arm from the chain stay (frame).

Tools you may need

Before you ride, use a good tire pressure gauge to make sure your tires are properly inflated

Some tires are a tight fit on the rim - to remove them, you'll need a set of tire levers

When replacing a tube, make sure the rim strip or tape covering the spoke nipples is in place and in good shape. It's a good idea to keep a roll of rim tape in your tool box (it's much more secure than the rubber rim strip)

Not so much a tool as a preventive measure, a tire sealant such as Slime will greatly reduce your chances of getting a flat tire

You'll need a set of cone wrenches if you're going to adjust your hub bearings - regular wrenches are too thick. Don't use cone wrenches for anything other than adjusting cones (they aren't designed for high-torque applications)

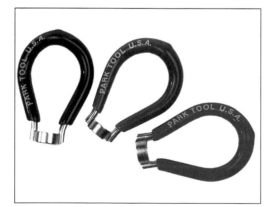

Never use anything other than a spoke wrench for adjusting spokes. Be sure to get the correct size for the spoke nipples on your wheel (universal spoke wrenches are also available that have slots for many different spoke nipple sizes)

A good degreaser is necessary for cleaning out old grease from the hub bearings

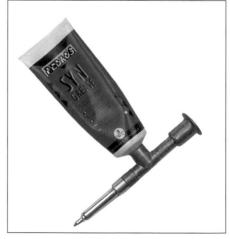

Use a good bicycle grease when lubricating hub bearings. Also, the grease injector shown here makes grease application quick and easy

 # Wheels, tires and hubs

Troubleshooting

Problem	Possible cause	Remedy
Bike feels shaky or wobbly	Loose hub bearings Headset bearings loose	Adjust the hub bearings Adjust the headset (see Chapter 11)
Bike doesn't coast well	Hub bearings worn or in need of service Brake pads rubbing on rim	Disassemble, inspect and clean the hub bearings, lubricate or replace as necessary Adjust brake (see Chapter 9)
Popping or clicking sounds while pedaling or coasting	Loose spokes	Tighten spokes and true-up wheel
Tires go flat repeatedly	Valve stem core loose Tires worn too thin Thorn stuck in tire Rim tape or strip missing or mispositioned, allowing spoke nipples to contact tube End of spoke protruding past nipple and contacting tube Air pressure in tire too low Too many hazards in your riding area	Tighten valve stem core Replace tires Remove tire, carefully check inside of tire for thorn Remove tire and tube, install or reposition rim tape or strip Install shorter spoke or file off excess from spoke end Inflate tires to proper pressure Install "Slime" or equivalent tube sealer in tubes
Wheel doesn't spin well or axles hard to turn (with wheel removed)	Hub bearings too tight Hub bearings in need of service	Adjust hub bearings Disassemble hub, clean and inspect hub and bearings, lubricate or replace as required
Wheel or axle feels "notchy" when turned slowly by hand	Hub bearings in need of service Hub bearings, hub and/or cones worn	Disassemble hub, clean and inspect hub and bearings, lubricate or replace as required Disassemble, clean and inspect hub and bearing components, lubricate or (most likely) replace hubs
Brake pad(s) rub on rim	Wheel out of true Brakes out of adjustment	True-up wheel Adjust brakes (see Chapter 9)
Bike surges or shakes when braking	Rim dented Wheel out of true	Repair or replace rim True-up wheel

1 Wheel removal and installation
(continued)

Tip:

If you're removing a rear wheel, shift the bike into high gear so the chain moves to the smallest rear sprocket. This will make removal of the wheel easier.

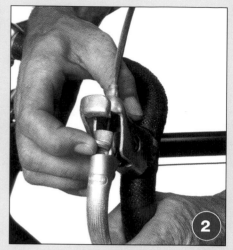

Release the brake to spread the pads apart, which will provide room for the tire to pass through. If your bike has side-pull brakes, flip the lever on the brake up.

If your bike has center-pull brakes, look on the brake lever for a small release lever - if it has one, push it. If it doesn't, see Photo 4).

If you have link-wire or straddle-cable cantilever brakes, detach the link wire or straddle cable from the brake arm.

If you have U-brakes or center-pull brakes without a release at the lever, detach the straddle cable from the yoke.

If the wheel is secured to the frame or forks with axle nuts, loosen the nuts enough to allow the axle to pass through the dropout (the slot in the frame or fork that the axle fits into). Use two wrenches, if possible, loosening the nuts at the same time an equal amount.

If your bike has quick-release axles, flip the quick release lever out. It might also be necessary to unscrew the nut on the other end of the quick release skewer a couple of turns to allow the axle to pass through the dropouts.

Wheels, tires and hubs

7

8

If you're removing the rear wheel on a multi-speed bike, look for a little protrusion on the right side seat stay, about three inches or so from the dropout. This is a chain hanger - if your bike has one of these, lift your chain up and hang it there. It will make wheel installation a little easier.

Remove the wheel. If you're taking off a rear wheel of a multi-speed bike, push the wheel forward and down, disengaging the chain from the sprocket. The derailleur will also spring forward, so you may have to angle the wheel sideways or pull the derailleur to the rear to get it out of the way.

Tire, tube and rim details

Tire

Tube

Rim

Rim tape

Spoke nipple

Spoke

1 Wheel removal and installation
(continued)

Installation

Installing the wheel is pretty much the reverse of removing it. If you're installing a rear wheel on a multi-speed bike, maneuver the wheel into position, making sure the chain engages with the smallest rear sprocket.

If there are washers on either side of the axle, make sure they are positioned on the outside of the dropouts on the frame or fork.

Tip:

Before installing the wheel, it's a good idea to check the hub bearings for play, tightness or grittiness. If necessary, service the hub bearings (see Section 3). (Hubs with quick-release axles should have a tiny amount of play in them when they aren't secured. When the quick-release lever is tightened, the play should disappear and the wheel should turn freely.)

When the wheel is in place, make sure it is completely seated in the dropout, align the wheel in the frame or fork, then tighten the axle nuts or quick-release lever. If you have a quick-release lever, you'll probably have to turn the nut on the opposite side of the lever clockwise a couple of turns, until most of the slack in the quick-release skewer (the rod that passes through the axle) is taken up. It should take quite a bit of effort to close the lever - enough to leave an imprint on your hand. Also, the CLOSE marking on the lever should be facing out (most quick-release levers are marked OPEN or CLOSE) and the lever should be positioned near the fork leg (front) or chain stay (rear) so it won't get caught on anything as you ride. **Photos 9 and 10**

If you're installing a rear wheel on a bike with coaster brakes, loop the chain over the sprocket and position the wheel in the frame. Pull the wheel back in the dropouts until you have a little chain slack - about 1/2-inch in the center of the chain. Connect the brake arm to the chainstay (don't tighten it yet) then align the wheel in the frame and tighten the axle nuts. Remember, if washers are present, they go between the nuts and the dropouts. Tighten the brake arm-to-chainstay fasteners.

On bikes with handbrakes, engage the brake release lever or connect the link wire or straddle cable.

Spin the wheel, making sure it rotates freely and the tire doesn't contact the frame or forks. Check the operation of the brakes, adjusting them if necessary (see Chapter 9).

9

10

Tire check

Always keep your tires properly inflated, as this will ensure proper handling of your bike and reduce the chances of damaged rims and flat tires. Check your tires for damage, too. A crack in the tread of a tire, especially on a high-pressure road bike tire, can result in a blowout.

2 Tube replacement

If you do much riding, this is a job that you'll probably be able to do with your eyes shut before too long. Unfortunately, flat tires are an all-too-common occurrence. On the bright side, tube replacement is a relatively easy operation and, with a little practice, one that won't keep you out of the saddle for very long.

Before beginning this procedure make sure you have a replacement tube of the proper size, and make sure it has the right kind of valve (Schrader, like a car tire, or Presta, a

Tip:

A tube with a Presta valve can be used with a rim drilled for a Schrader valve. The opposite is not true unless you drill out a Presta valve rim to accept the larger Schrader valve.

much narrower valve with a little nut on top that unscrews).You might also need a set of tire levers.

Remove the wheel (see Section 1 if necessary) and unscrew the cap on the valve stem. If the tube has just been punctured and still has some air in it, depress the valve stem core and let all of the air out. If your tube has a Presta valve you'll have to unscrew the small nut at the top of the valve first.

Unseat the tire bead from the rim (do this on one side of the tire only). This can be done by hand on many tires, especially large ones like mountain bike tires. If possible, work the bead of the tire over the rim until the entire bead on one side of the tire is off the rim.

If the tire is a tight fit on the rim and you can't get it off by hand, you'll have to use tire levers. Insert the blade of one tire lever between the tire bead and the rim, then pry it back to raise the tire bead above the lip of the rim. If your levers have hooks on the ends, attach the lever to one of the spokes to keep it in place.

Insert another tire lever between the tire and rim approximately three or four inches from the first. Pull back on the lever - at this point you'll probably be able to slide this lever around the rim and unseat the tire. If the tire is a really tight fit, you may need one more lever.

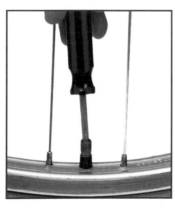

Tip

Before replacing a tube, check the valve stem core for a leak by removing the cap and applying a little water or saliva to the valve. Hold your finger over the valve - if bubbles appear, the valve stem core is leaking. It may be possible to tighten the core and eliminate the leak. A special wrench is required to do this on Schrader valve cores (some valve stem caps have two small prongs on top for this purpose). Presta valves have a small nut on top that may loosen up, but they usually don't leak.

2 Tube replacement
(continued)

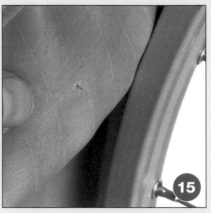

With one side of the tire unseated from the rim, push the valve stem through the rim and pull the tube out of the tire. If you want to patch it, refer to the accompanying sidebar *"Tube Repair."*

Carefully check the inside of the tire for thorns and pebbles. Also make sure the rim strip (the tape or rubber piece that covers the spoke nipples) is in place.

Using your pump, partially inflate the new tube just enough for it to hold a circular shape.

Insert the tube between the tire and the rim, beginning with the valve stem. Push the valve stem through the hole in the rim, making sure it is straight.

Tuck the tube into the rest of the tire, being careful not to twist it or pinch it between the tire bead on the other side.

Once the tube is inside the tire, begin mounting the tire on the rim. Extreme care must be taken so as not to pinch the tube between the rim and the tire bead. If possible, use your hands only. If you had to use tire levers to pull the tire bead over the rim, it'll probably be necessary to use them to remount the tire. If so, be careful not to catch the tube with the lever, or you'll probably put a hole in it. Also, never use a screwdriver to remount the tire bead. The chances of ruining the tube are much greater (and you could also put a nick in the rim).

After you've mounted the tire on the rim, check for bulges or bumps in the tire sidewall, which would indicate the tube is not properly situated. It's usually possible to "massage" the area with your thumbs to persuade the tube into place.

See if the valve stem is straight. If it isn't, work the tire and tube one way or the other until it is.

Now, inflate the tube with your pump. As you do this, make sure the tire beads seat properly and the tube doesn't make any bulges in the sidewall.

Tip:

On some tires, particularly the looser-fitting mountain bike tires, it's a good idea to make sure that the tire tread is centered on the rim. Just check that the reinforced bead area on each side of the tire is protruding equally from the rim. If it isn't, you'll have to even up this protrusion before adding more air.

Inflate the tire to the pressure marked on the tire sidewall. Hold the wheel by the axle ends and spin it, checking to make sure the tire is properly seated and there are no bumps or bulges.

Install the wheel (see Section 1).

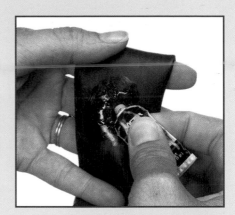

Tube repair

Replacing the inner tube is the quickest and most favorable way to rectify a flat tire. You should know how to patch a tube, however, especially if you ride long distances or off-road. You should always carry a spare tube and a patch kit. If you flat, replace the tube and save the old one for a spare. If you flat again, you'll have two potential spares, one of which you'll fix right

Note: 1

If the leak is coming from the base of the valve stem, throw the tube away - don't even try to fix it.

Note: 2

Some patch kits are "glueless;" the adhesive on the patch is enough to keep it stuck to the tube.

away so you can resume your ride.

You'll need a bicycle tube patch kit and a pump for this job.

1 Remove the tube as described in Section 2.

2 Partially inflate the tube with your pump and search for the leak. When you find the leak, circle it with a piece of chalk or a marking pen if one is available.

3 Once you've found the leak, let most of the air out of the tube. Using a piece of sandpaper from the patch kit, or the lid of the patch kit (some have a small "cheese grater" type lid) roughen-up the area over and around the hole. This will help the patch stick better.

4 Smear a thin, even film of glue over and around the area of the hole. The glue should extend beyond the area where the patch will lay.

5 Allow the glue to "set up" for a couple of minutes, until it turns from shiny and wet-looking to a dull and hazy cast. Peel the foil backing off the patch and press the patch into place.

Squeeze the tube, with your thumbs pushing down on the patch, working from the middle of the patch to the outside.

6 Peel off the thin plastic or paper cover from the patch and sprinkle a little talcum powder or very fine dust on the patch and surrounding area. This will prevent the glue from adhering to the inside of the tire.

7 Install the tube in the tire (see Section 2) or fold it up and put it in your tool bag.

TIP

If you carry a spare tube, which you should, carry one with a Presta valve even if your bike uses tubes with Schrader valves (Presta valves will fit rims drilled for Schrader valves, but a Schrader valve won't fit in a Presta valve hole). This way, if one of your riding partners gets a flat and needs a tube, they can use your spare Presta valve tube no matter which kind they presently have.

Presta

Schrader

Tire replacement

Replacing a tire isn't much more involved than installing a new tube. Refer to Section 2 and remove the tube from the tire, then pull the bead of the tire that's still on the rim off the same side of the rim that the first bead was removed from.

Before installing the tire, look for markings on the sidewall indicating the proper direction of rotation, making sure you mount the tire on the rim so the directional arrow points the right way (not all tires have directional markings).

Install one side of the tire on the rim, then refer to Section 2, install the tube and complete the tire mounting process.

Hub bearing check

You can quickly check the adjustment of your hub bearings by shaking the wheel side-to-side - any play in the bearings can be felt easily using this method

Hub details

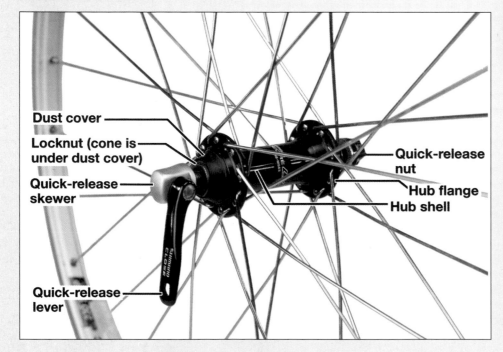

Dust cover

Locknut (cone is under dust cover)

Quick-release skewer

Quick-release lever

Quick-release nut

Hub flange

Hub shell

3 Hub bearing maintenance

The bearings in your hubs are subjected to incredible loads, mostly radially but also laterally. When these bearings get out of adjustment or dirty, the shape of the bearings become distorted after some time, and the races get ruined, too. It's important to keep these bearings adjusted properly and to service them regularly (every six months or so) to ensure their cleanliness.

3a Adjustment

Occasionally you'll find it necessary to adjust your hub bearings, usually because they become a little sloppy but sometimes because they're too tight and the wheel doesn't spin freely.

If only a minor adjustment is necessary, you'll only have to adjust the cones on one side of the hub. If you're adjusting the bearings on the rear wheel, work only on the left side (the side without the sprockets).

Begin by removing the wheel from the bike (see Section 1 if necessary).

If the bike you're working on has axle nuts instead of quick releases, it may be possible to loosen up the nut on one side of the axle only, leaving the opposite side tight and the wheel in place (if your wrenches are thin enough you can sometimes get away with this).

Once adjusted, reinstall the dust cover, if equipped, and mount the wheel on the bike. If you have quick-release hubs, tighten them up and make sure the wheel spins freely, but that there also is no slop in the bearings.

Remove the dust covers if your hub is equipped with them. (If the hub does have dust covers, you'll have to remove the axle nut from one side or, if you have quick-release hubs, remove the quick-release skewer).

Holding the cone steady with a cone wrench, loosen up the locknut by turning it counterclockwise.

Holding the opposite end of the axle with your other hand, turn the cone in or out, as necessary, to adjust the hub bearings. If your hub has axle nuts instead of quick releases, take out all of the play but don't preload the bearings (the axle should turn freely but you shouldn't be able to feel any slop when you wiggle the axle). If you have quick-release axles, adjust the cones so the bearings have a little bit of play in them. When the quick release is tightened, the axle will be compressed slightly and the play will disappear. It may take a few tries to get the adjustment right. When you're satisfied with the adjustment, hold the cone with the cone wrench and tighten the locknut securely. Recheck the adjustment. If tightening the locknut caused the adjustment to change, repeat the procedure and move the cone in or out, as necessary, to compensate for the change that takes place when the locknut is tightened.

If you keep messing up the adjustment when you tighten the locknut, mount the opposite locknut in the jaws of a vise, with the wheel horizontal, and *tighten the vise only enough to prevent the axle from turning.* The jaws of the vise must only contact the flats of the locknut. Now repeat the adjustment procedure and tighten the locknut.

3 Hub bearing maintenance (continued)

3b Hub bearing overhaul

Every six months (or more often if you submerge your hubs in water) the hubs should be disassembled, cleaned, inspected and lubricated. If wear is noticed or the axle felt gritty when turned, the bearings and cones and, if the hub races are pitted, the entire hub should be replaced, too. The cleaning and lubricating procedure is only slightly more involved than adjusting the hubs.

Before you begin this job, make sure you have some good bicycle bearing grease and some type of degreaser (preferably of the citrus-based variety).

Remove the wheel from the bike (see Section 1 if necessary).

Remove the axle nuts or, if you have quick-release axles, remove the quick-release skewer. This is done by unscrewing the conical nut on the skewer, opposite the lever. Pull the skewer through the axle, being careful not to lose the two springs.

Remove the dust caps if your hubs are equipped with them. At this stage, follow photos 23 through 29 for the overhaul procedure.

Once the axle is reinstalled, refer to the *Adjustment* procedure and adjust the hub bearings. Don't forget to tighten the locknut securely and install the dust cover, if so equipped.

Install the wheel, referring to Section 1 if necessary.

Note: *If you're overhauling the hub on a rear wheel and you have a screw-on freewheel, remove the freewheel (see Chapter 8).*

Remove the locknut from one side of the axle, holding the cone on the other side with a cone wrench to prevent it from turning.

Remove the washer (if present) and the cone from the axle.

Pull the axle out of the hub from the opposite side. The bearings will most likely stay in the hub, but be prepared to catch them if they do spill out.

Using a small screwdriver or a magnet, remove the bearings from their races. Count how many bearings are in each side of the hub - each race should contain the same amount. Place the bearings in a small container or on a rag so they can't roll away.

Wash all of the parts with degreaser - a film canister partially filled with degreaser makes a great bearing washer. Check the axle to make sure it's straight. Carefully inspect the bearing contact area on the cones and the races in the hub for pitting and other signs of wear. Also check the ball bearings for pitting. Replace any worn parts with new ones. If the races in the hub are pitted, you'll have to take the wheel to a bike shop and have a new hub laced into your rim, or just buy a new wheel.

Note 1:

Don't unscrew the locknut and the cone from the axle unless the axle or the cone must be replaced (this will make assembly easier). If it is necessary to remove this cone and locknut, measure the distance from the end of the axle to the locknut and be sure to thread the cone and locknut back on the same distance from the axle end during assembly.

Note 2:

If new parts are necessary, take the old ones with you to the bike shop so you can match them up.

Apply a generous bead of grease to each hub race.

Install the ball bearings into the races, pushing them into the grease. Apply a little more grease over the tops of the bearings. Guide the axle through the hub, being careful not to disturb the bearings, then thread the cone, washer (if equipped) and locknut onto the other side (don't tighten the locknut until the hub bearings have been adjusted).

Warning:

If you have quick-release axles, make sure each end of the axle fits into the dropouts in the frame or fork but be certain that neither side protrudes past the dropout. If it does protrude, the wheel won't be adequately secured when the quick release is tightened. If necessary, loosen the locknuts on each side of the axle and adjust the cones as necessary to center the axle in the hub. Recheck to make sure the axle doesn't protrude past either dropout.

3 Hub bearing maintenance
(continued)

Hub lubrication

Some hubs have a small hole in the cover over each bearing and one in the center of the hub, between the flanges. These hubs can be lubricated periodically without disassembling them by inserting the tip of a grease injector into each hole and applying a few pumps of grease. The hole in the center of the hub is concealed by a spring steel cover which must be slid out of the way for access to the hole. Be sure to slide the cover back into place when you're done.

4 Spoke replacement

The bicycle wheel is an amazing structure. Each individual component of the wheel could be considered rather frail, until they are all laced together and the spokes properly tensioned. Then the wheel is almost capable of taking any kind of punishment we can dish out.

Aside from the material and construction of the rim, the key to a strong wheel lies in the tension of the spokes. When spokes are too tight they overly stress the rim - one hard blow to the rim can cause it to fold up like a taco shell. Loose spokes also result in a weak wheel. When this happens, the rim must take too many forces and will no doubt become out of true and will most likely bend.

Another common malady is spoke breakage. When a spoke breaks the wheel immediately goes out of true, and the errant spoke can take more with it as the wheel turns. If this happens on the road or out on the trail and you don't have a replacement spoke, try to remove the pieces. If the broken spoke is on the freewheel side of the rear wheel you might not be able to remove it. In this case wrap the remnant of the spoke around an adjacent spoke, then take your spoke wrench and loosen the spokes on each side of the broken spoke 1/2-turn.

1   To replace the spoke, begin by removing the tube from the tire (see Section 2), then remove the tire from the rim (this will make it easier to true-up the rim). Peel back the rim strip, pull out the spoke nipple and section of broken spoke. If the broken spoke is on the drive (freewheel) side of the rear wheel, the freewheel or freehub sprockets will have to be removed (see Chapter 8). **Photo 30**

2   Remove one of the good spokes (make sure it's from the same side of the hub if you're working on a rear wheel). Take it to the bike shop so you can be sure you'll get the correct length and gauge replacement.

3   Insert the new spoke through its hole in the hub, in the opposite direction of the spokes flanking the empty hole. Look at the way the surrounding spokes cross over and under each other - make sure the new spoke crosses over or under its companion spokes the way it's supposed to.

4   Thread the nipple onto the spoke and tighten it just enough to put some tension on the spoke. Try to match the tension to that of the other spokes.

5   True-up the rim by following the procedure outlined in Section 6.

6   Install the tire and tube (see Section 2) and mount the wheel on the bike (see Section 1 if necessary).

Note:
It's a good idea to install a new nipple, too.

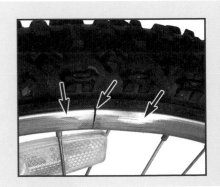

5 Rim replacement

Building a wheel from scratch is kind of tricky and won't be covered in this manual. Really, it's a job for a bike shop. But replacing a damaged rim can be accomplished fairly easily using the following method. For this procedure you'll need a new rim, replacement spokes and/or nipples if any were damaged, and a roll of tape (any kind will do, as long as it peels off without leaving a sticky mess to clean up). Final truing of the wheel should be left to a bike shop, but lacing up the wheel by following this procedure should save you some labor charges.

1   Remove the damaged wheel from the bike and dismount the tire, tube and rim strip. Remove the freewheel assembly or freehub sprockets if you're replacing the rear rim. Obtain a new rim of the correct size, making sure it has the same number of spoke holes as the old one, and the hole for the valve stem is the right size for your

Rim damage

Check your rims frequently for damage like this. Dents, dings and bulges can sometimes be straightened out, but such repairs are usually performed as a temporary fix just to get home. Splits in the rim are potentially very dangerous, as they can lead to sudden collapse of the wheel. It's best not to ride on a rim with a split seam.

preference of valve stem type (Presta or Schrader).

2   Take the new rim and set it on the damaged one, aligning the holes for the valve stem. Make sure the stagger of the spoke holes in the new rim match those of the bent one (the holes are offset to one side or the other). When all of the holes are properly aligned, tape the rims together in this position. Two or three strips of tape should be adequate. **Photo 31**

3   Loosen all of the spoke nipples about three turns so the wheel is very "loose." Now fully unscrew one spoke nipple from a spoke on the side of the hub nearest the new rim, slide the spoke out of the bent rim and insert it into the corresponding hole in the new rim. Lubricate the end of the spoke with grease and thread the nipple onto the spoke. **Photo 32**

4   Move on to the next spoke coming from the same side of the hub as the first spoke was transplanted from and repeat this procedure. On the rim side, this means you'll skip a spoke, moving to the second one in line.

5   Once you've worked your way around the rim, transferring all of the spokes from the near side of the hub, start moving the spokes from the far side of the hub. **Photo 33**

6   After all of the spokes have been moved and the hub is suspended sloppily somewhere near the center of the new rim, remove the tape and detach the old rim. Begin tightening the

Note:

The rim should be centered on the axle when viewed from the end. On the front wheel this is easy to verify, as the hub flanges serve as a good reference point. On rear wheels of most multi-speed bikes it can be a little deceiving because the wheel "dish" is not symmetrical. The spokes on the drive (sprocket) side of the hub are usually a little shorter than the ones on the non-drive side (and tensioned about twice as tight). The drive side of the hub is closer to the center line of the bike to make room for the sprockets.

spoke nipples until the spokes just begin to take on a little tension. This can be verified by mounting the axle in the dropouts and wiggling the rim from side-to-side. If the spoke nipples rise and fall in their holes in the rim, the spokes are still loose.

7   At this stage it is best to take the rim to a bike shop to have the spokes properly tensioned and the wheel trued. Without having this done you run the risk of destroying your new rim (and possibly hurting yourself).

6 Wheel truing

It's important to periodically check your wheels for wobbles or bumps in the rim as you rotate it slowly. Distortions like these are usually from hitting objects on the road or trail and most often will result in a few loose spokes. On the other hand, spokes that are too loose can allow these kinds of rim distortions to occur.

Minor wobbles can usually be ironed out by a little judicious spoke tightening (and sometimes loosening). However, the following procedure is in no way intended to be a complete, precision wheel-truing guide. It is simply a method of straightening out or reducing minor wheel imperfections. Keep in mind that a wheel that is overly stressed by spoke tightening is probably more dangerous than a wheel with loose spokes. Don't overdo it with the spoke wrench!

1   Before attempting to true the wheel, check for loose spokes. They should all have about the same amount of tension on them. Squeeze each pair of spokes on one side of the hub between your thumb and your index finger. Each set should offer the same amount of resistance to movement. Using a spoke wrench, tighten up any spokes that are obviously loose. Check the spokes on the other hub, too. **Photo 34**

2   Support the bike on a workstand if possible, or turn it over and stand it on its seat and handlebars (if neces-

sary, place a couple of two-by-fours under the bars so the shifters don't get damaged).

3   Hold a piece of chalk or a marking pen about 1/4-inch away from the rim, bracing your hand against a brake lever, fork leg or seat stay. Slowly spin the wheel and see if the rim contacts the chalk or pen. If it doesn't, move the chalk or pen a little closer to the rim. At some point the rim will contact the chalk or pen if it is out of true. The resulting mark on the rim will indicate a sideways deflection. **Photo 35**

4   Note where the mark is in relation to the spokes. If the mark is directly over a spoke that goes to the hub flange on the opposite side, that spoke should be tightened 1/2-turn, and the spokes on either side of that one should each be loosened 1/4-turn. **Photo 36**

5   Wipe off the rim and repeat the

check. If the deflection is still there, tighten the spoke a little more and loosen the spokes on either side a little, too. Always work in small increments.

6   If the bend is very gradual and involves a number of spokes, loosen the spokes that travel to the hub flange on the same side of the rim you're checking, and tighten the spokes that go to the opposite side. In principle it's easy - loosen near-side spokes, tighten far-side spokes. In practice this can be maddening if the wheel is really out of whack.

7   A wheel that requires excessive tightening and loosening of the spokes to get it into shape should be taken to a bike shop for professional truing.

Rim repair

Minor bulges, dings, bends and out-of-round conditions in a rim can sometimes be straightened out with a little force. While any rim that is severely damaged should be replaced, these tricks can sometimes make the difference between riding your bike home or carrying it. Just keep in mind that these are crude, temporary repairs.

Bulges

Bulges occur when you hit a solid object while traveling too fa or with underinflated tires. Usually they come in pairs - one on each side of the rim.

Remove the wheel from the bike and let the air out of the tire. Position the damaged portion of the rim on a flat surface (a curb, log or fence post) and, using a soft-face hammer (if one is available), strike the bulge hard enough to flatten it down flush with the rest of the rim. If there's a bulge on the other side of the rim, flip it over and repeat the procedure. If you don't have the luxury of a soft-face hammer, use a piece of two-by-four or a nice, smooth rock.

It may be necessary to spread the edges of the rim if you used a little too much force. Refer to the Dings procedure to pull out the depressed areas of the rim.

You should also check the tightness of the spokes in the vicinity of the former bulge, tightening them up as necessary. Inflate the tire and resume your ride.

Dings

Minor dings can be removed by dismounting the tire and using an adjustable wrench, placed over the lip of the rim, as a lever. Bend the rim out a little at a time, working in different spots on the bend, so as not to over-stretch the metal. It's a good idea to check the spoke tension under the damaged area when you're done.

Warning: *If you notice any cracks or splits in the rim, don't ride on it - carry or push your bike home. It's not worth the risk.*

Bends

Remove the wheel from the bike. Hold the wheel with both hands and, with the bowed portion of the rim resting against a solid object, push down with enough force to bend the rim back into shape. Some of the spokes will most likely have to be tightened. Refer to Section 6 and true up the wheel as best as you can.

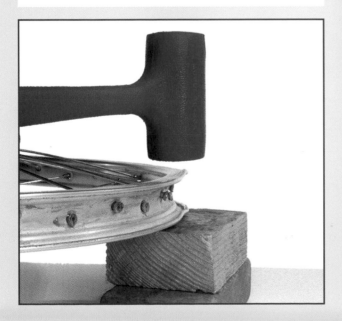

Rim repair (continued)

Out-of-round condition

If you've impacted something really hard and flat-spotted one of your rims (this usually happens to the front wheel) this procedure sometimes works. Remove the wheel from the bike and find a strong stick or a two-by-four (if you use something as large as a two-by-four you'll have to take off the tire and remove a couple of spokes over the damaged area). Stand the wheel up with the damaged portion of the rim on the ground. Place the stick or two-by-four over the depressed area, straddle the rim and stand on the wood. Pull up with as much effort as it takes to remove the kink in the rim.

Reinstall the spokes and true-up the rim as best as you can. Install the tire and tube.

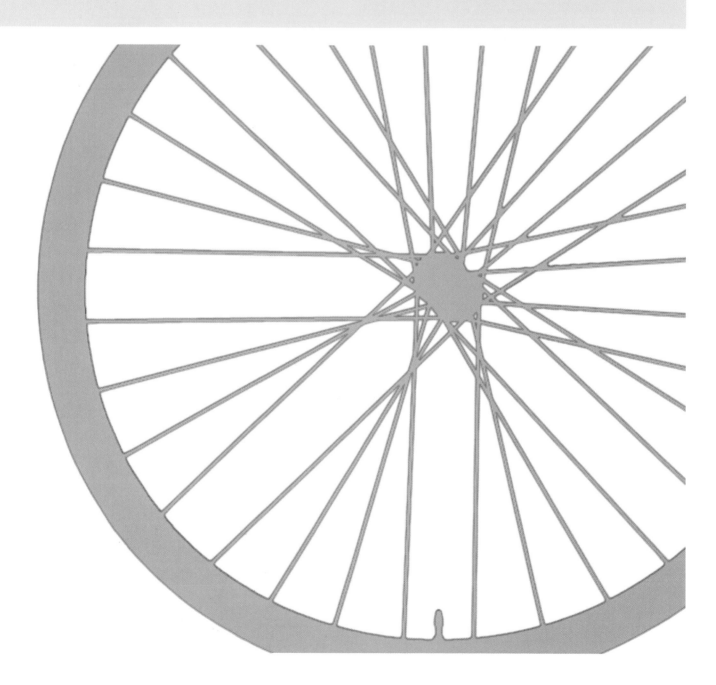

5

Crankset and pedals

Chainring bolt

Chainring

Crank arm bolt

Crank arm

Pedal (clipless)

5 Crankset and pedals

Contents

Introduction

This Chapter covers the front half of the power transmission to the rear wheel: the pedals, cranks and bottom bracket.

Although most bicycles manufactured these days are equipped with individual crank arms connected to an axle supported by the bottom bracket bearings, this chapter also includes service procedures for one-piece cranks, commonly found on single-speeds and older American bikes.

1 Chainrings

1a Inspection and maintenance

Chainrings are the large "sprockets" bolted to the right side crank arm. Some bikes only have one, some have as many as three. They usually don't require any attention other than checking to make sure the bolts are tight. They can wear out or become damaged, however.

The chainring teeth can be easily checked for wear and damage. Wear occurs from normal usage of the bike, although a neglected chain can accelerate wear. Damage occurs when the chainring (almost always the large one) contacts a rock or other object on the ground.

Note:
Some chainrings use teeth of varying profiles to aid in shifting - don't confuse these teeth with worn-out ones.

Tools you may need

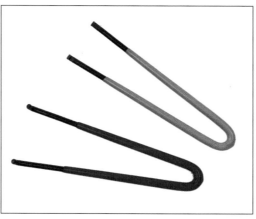

You'll need a crank puller if you plan to remove the crank arms from the bottom bracket spindle. Don't ever try to use a hammer to knock them off!

While not absolutely necessary, a special pedal wrench like this offers plenty of leverage for unscrewing tight or seized pedals

A universal crank nut/bolt wrench like this will prevent you from making more than one trip to your tool box - all three common sizes are included, so you don't have to worry about guessing wrong

A lockring spanner will be necessary to loosen the lockring on the left side bearing cup of an adjustable bottom bracket. The other end of the wrench is used for unscrewing the stationary cup on the right side of the bottom bracket shell

To service an adjustable bottom bracket you'll probably need a special spanner like one of these

For removing and installing cartridge bottom brackets, a special spline-drive tool is required

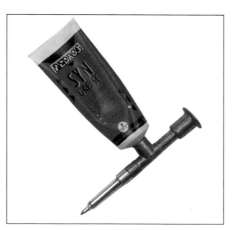

Whenever you service the bottom bracket or pedal bearings, a good degreaser will be necessary to remove the old grease from the components

Use bicycle grease when lubricating bottom bracket or pedal bearings. The grease injector shown here makes grease application quick and easy

Anti-seize can be used on the bottom bracket spindle where the crank arms mount - this will prevent the crank arms from "freezing" to the spindle and ease future removal. It can also be used on bottom bracket threads (and should be used if you're installing a titanium bottom bracket). Be careful not to get any on your skin, as it contains lead

Troubleshooting

Problem	Possible cause	Remedy
Bike is hard to pedal (but coasts okay)	Bottom bracket bearings misadjusted, worn or in need of service	Disassemble, clean and inspect the bottom bracket (non-cartridge type), lubricate or replace as necessary
Clicking, popping, squeaking or creaking noises while pedaling only	Pedal(s) loose on crank arm(s)	Tighten the pedal(s)
	Pedal bearings dry or worn	Disassemble pedal (if possible), inspect pedal bearings, lubricate or replace as necessary
	Pedal cage loose on pedal	Tighten pedal cage screws
	Loose toe-clip fasteners	Tighten toe-clip fasteners
	Loose chainring bolts	Tighten chainring bolts
	Loose crank arm(s)	Tighten crank arm bolt(s) or nut(s). If it's still loose, the crank arm(s) may be worn out.
	Spot weld on chainring broken (non-removable chainrings)	Replace crankset
	Bottom bracket bearings worn, dry or out of adjustment (non-cartridge type)	Disassemble, clean and inspect bottom bracket, lubricate and adjust or replace as required
	Bottom bracket loose in frame or worn (cartridge type)	Tighten or replace bottom bracket as necessary
	Chain worn out	Replace chain (and inspect sprockets and chainrings replacing parts as necessary (see Chapter 8)
	Chainring(s) worn or bent/dented	Straighten bent chainring teeth if possible, or replace chainring(s)
Chainrings worn	Normal wear	Replace chainring(s)
	Worn-out chain	Replace chain and chainrings (see Chapter 8)
Chainring rubs against front derailleur	Chainring bent	Straighten or replace chainring
	Crank arm spider bent	Replace crank arm
Cranks hard to turn or are noisy	Bottom bracket bearings in need of service or are noisy or are worn out	Disassemble, clean and inspect bottom bracket, replacing or relubing as required (non-cartridge type) or replace bottom bracket (cartridge type)
Pedal wobbles on spindle	Loose or worn pedal bearings	Adjust pedal bearings, if possible, or replace pedals
Pedals don't turn freely on spindle	Pedal bearings too tight	Adjust pedal bearings, if possible, or replace pedals
	Pedal bearings in need of service	Disassemble, clean and inspect pedal bearings (if possible), lubricate and reassemble pedals

1 Chainrings
(continued)

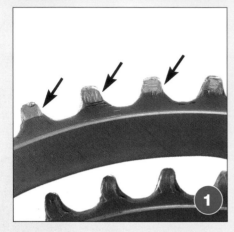

1

There are two types of wear - shift wear and load wear. If the chainring teeth suffer from load wear, the drive side of the teeth (the front side of the teeth when they're at the top of chainring rotation) will appear "steeper" than the other side of the teeth.

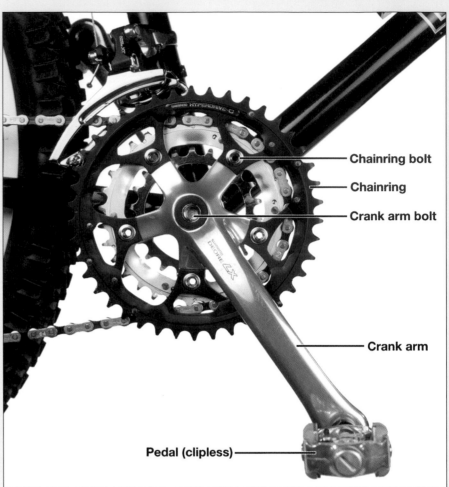

Chainring bolt

Chainring

Crank arm bolt

Crank arm

Pedal (clipless)

2

Shift wear is much more common and results in the sides of the chainring teeth rounding off and thinning out. It occurs mostly on the middle chainring.

3

Damage to the chainring teeth can sometimes be repaired by straightening the teeth with a pair of pliers or an adjustable wrench.

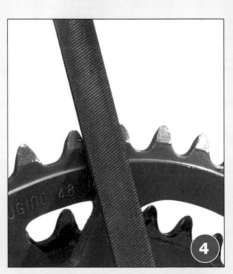

4

If the teeth are jagged (from grinding against rocks) they can be smoothed-out with a little careful filing.

1b Replacement

Note that some chainrings on bikes with lower-end component groups are spot-welded or riveted together and are not replaceable. These types of chainrings must be replaced as a set, along with the crank arms (see Section 3). Or, if you can afford it, upgrade your crankset to one that accepts individual chainrings.

To replace the chainring on a single-speed bike with one-piece cranks, refer to the procedure described in Section 4a.4, as it is necessary to disassemble the bottom bracket and remove the crank to detach the chainring.

Note:

Some index shift systems have markings on the backsides of the chainrings. These markings must be installed in the 12 o'clock position when the drive-side crankarm is in the 6 o'clock position. Also, the chain drop pin on the large chainring must be situated over the drive-side crank arm.

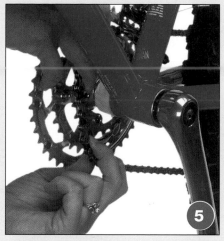

5

Remove the chain from the chainring that is to be replaced. On multi-speed bikes this can be done by simply lifting the chain off the chainring (s) and laying it on the bottom bracket shell (or another chainring). It's a good idea to place a rag or a piece of tape over the bottom bracket shell so the paint doesn't get scratched. If you're working on a single-speed bike with detachable crankarms, loosen the rear axle nuts and move the rear wheel forward to provide enough slack in the chain to allow removal. If you are only going to remove the inner chainring from a triple-ring crankset, skip to Photo 10.

6

Mark the relationship of the chainrings to the crank arm. If you're going to reinstall the same rings, be sure to align these marks when you put them back on. Unscrew the bolts that secure the chainring(s) together, turning them in the normal, counterclockwise direction. Most late model bikes have 5 mm Allen bolts securing the chainrings. These are usually pretty tight, so you might have to use a "cheater pipe" on the wrench for extra leverage. Be prepared for the nut on the inside of the middle chainring (or inner chainring on two-ring setups) to fall out.

Chainring care

The tightness of the chainring bolts should be checked frequently. If you ride hard daily, it's a good idea to check them daily.

Also, keep your chainrings clean - by doing so you'll increase the lifespan of your chainrings and your chain.

1 Chainrings
(continued)

When purchasing replacement chainrings, take the old ones with you to the bike shop. This way you'll be sure to get chainrings with the same bolt circle diameter.

Install the chainring(s) by reversing the disassembly process.

Note:

Put a thin film of grease on the threads of the chainring bolts to prevent them from "freezing up" over time, but don't allow grease to get on the outside of the nut, as these nuts need some traction where they seat so they don't spin as the bolt is tightened. Be sure to reinstall any washers or spacers in their proper positions, and tighten the chainring bolts securely.

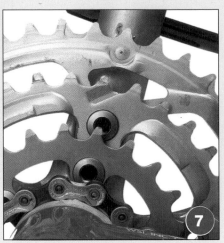

On some triple-ring cranksets the crank arm covers one of the outer chainring bolts. You'll notice that access to this bolt must be gained from the other side of the crankset. You may also find that a tooth on the inner ring makes it impossible to insert an Allen wrench into the bolt. If this is the case, you'll have to first remove the bolts from the inner ring and reposition it to make wrench placement possible.

Lift off the outer chainring. On three-ring setups, check for the presence of spacers or washers between the outer chainring and the middle chainring. Don't lose any of these if your crankset uses them.

Two-ring setups usually have thin washers between the inner chainring and the crank arm spider. Don't lose these either.

To remove the inner chainring from a triple-ring setup, refer to Section 3 and remove the right-side crank arm. Now, unscrew the bolts from the inside of the crankset that secure the inner ring.

2 Pedals

Pedal problems rarely go unnoticed. When troubles arise here they are not only heard, they are usually felt, often in the form of general looseness, clicking, popping and grating.

Pedal bearings are very busy components of your bike and subject to all kinds of harsh conditions. If they're not operating up to par they will sap your energy and make your ride less than pleasant. Every six months (or more often if you routinely ride through lots of water) you should disassemble your pedals and inspect them, cleaning and repacking the bearings if possible, or replacing them.

2a Removal and installation

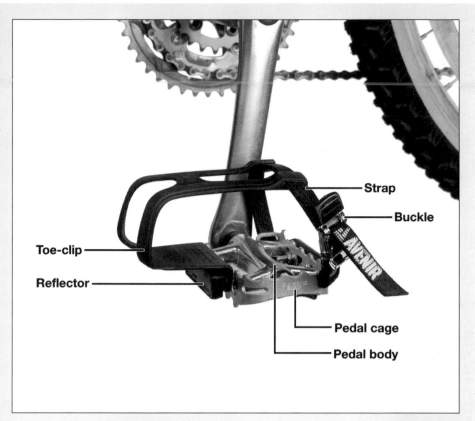

Toe-clip

Reflector

Strap

Buckle

Pedal cage

Pedal body

11

Before attempting to remove the pedals, spray some penetrating oil where the pedal spindle meets the crank arm. Also apply some from the other side so the oil can soak into the threads there, too. Let the penetrant work for a few minutes, then try to unscrew the pedals.

Tip: *If the pedal is very tight, try using a "cheater pipe" placed over the end of the wrench for extra leverage. Take the bike to a shop if it still won't come loose. Also, don't be too surprised if the steel spindle of the pedal pulls out some aluminum threads from the crank arm (even if you did turn it in the correct direction). This is not uncommon, but it does mean you'll have to replace the crank arm (and the pedal).*

12

Unscrew the pedals from the crank arms. The important thing to remember about pedal removal is that the left-side pedal has left-hand threads and the right-side pedal has right-hand threads. This means that you have to turn the left pedal spindle clockwise to unscrew it. The right side pedal unscrews in the conventional counterclockwise direction. One easy way to accustom yourself to this is to make sure the wrench is pointing up when you put it on the pedal spindle, then turn the wrench towards the rear of the bike - no matter which pedal you're removing.

13

When reinstalling the pedals, apply grease (or better yet, anti-seize compound) to the threads of the pedal spindle and the threads of the crank. Screw the pedal spindle into the crank arm by hand at first, so as not to strip any threads. Remember to turn the left-side pedal counterclockwise, as if you were loosening a standard fastener. Tighten the pedals with a wrench, but don't overdo it (just get them secure).

2 Pedals
(continued)

2b Pedal bearing overhaul and adjustment

Overhaul

It's important to make sure the pedal bearings are smothered with grease, but the only way to really ensure this is to take the pedal apart. Some pedals, however, are sealed and can't be disassembled. Other types of pedals could theoretically be taken apart, in that they have a regular cone secured by a locknut, but it is so difficult to get any kind of wrench or socket on the locknut that it just isn't worth the trouble. If you have either of these types of pedals it is best to just install new ones (but you won't know until you attempt the following procedure, so read on).

Note:
It may be helpful to remove any toe clips, straps and reflectors before overhauling the pedals.

14

With the pedals removed from the crank arms, remove the screws and detach the pedal cage from the pedal body.

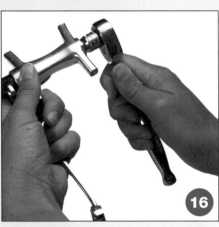

16

Hold the pedal spindle with a wrench (usually 15 mm) on the flats and, using a socket (usually 12 mm) unscrew the locknut.

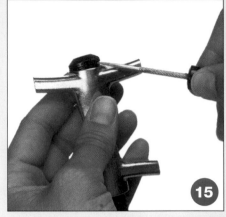

15

Pry off or unscrew the dust cap from the end of the pedal.

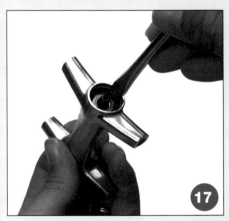

17

Take a small screwdriver and wedge it between the pedal bearing cone and the pedal body. Turn the pedal spindle with your other hand and the cone should unscrew up the spindle. Remove the washer (if one is present) and the cone, but be careful not to let the spindle come out of the pedal body.

Pedal bearing check

To check your pedal bearings, turn the pedal and feel for rough spots or grittiness. If they don't feel smooth, you'll have to overhaul the bearings or replace the pedals. Also try to move the pedal in-and-out - you shouldn't be able to feel any play in this direction. If you can, adjust the pedal bearings.

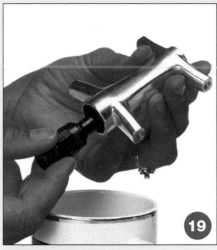

18 Pour the bearings out into a cup. If necessary, fish them out with a small screwdriver. Count how many there are.

19 Now pull out the spindle and let the remaining bearings fall into the cup. Count how many bearings come out of this side.

20 Apply a bead of grease to the bearing races in the pedal housing.

Cleaning

Clean all of the balls, the cone, spindle and pedal housing with degreaser and inspect for evidence of wear. Look for pitted areas on the cone, axle and on the races in the pedal housing, as well as damaged ball bearings. If the cone, axle and races are okay but the ball bearings are worn, you can get away with replacing the balls alone (take the old ones with you to the bike shop when you go to get new ones). If the races, axle or cone are worn, you'll probably have to replace the pedals.

Alternatives to toeclips and straps

If you avoid the traditional toe-clips and straps because you're afraid you won't be able to get your feet out of them quickly enough, you should consider using some other type of foot retention system. Shown here are two alternatives - Power Grips and clipless pedals. Power Grips securely attach your feet to the pedals, are easy to get out of, and don't require special shoes. When properly adjusted they will give you the same effect as toe-clips and straps.

Clipless pedals require special shoes, but are the safest way for you to maximize your pedaling effort. Once you're clipped in you can spin as fast as you are able, pull up on the pedals on the upstroke and perform bunny-hops like you never thought possible! All you have to do to free your foot is move your heel outward. The clipless pedals shown here are by Onza.

2 Pedals
(continued)

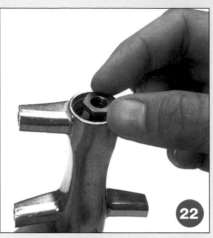

21 Press the bearings into the grease in each race. A pair of tweezers works fine for this step. Install the same number of bearings that came out - there should be enough to fill the race, but not so many that it causes one to "bulge" out of line. Install the spindle into the pedal body, being careful not to disturb the bearings. Make sure the rubber seal (if equipped) is in place, and that you are inserting the spindle into the correct side of the pedal body.

If the spindle does not turn freely, or feels loose, use a screwdriver to hold the cone stationary while you turn the spindle one way or the other.

22 Holding the pedal in a vertical position, screw the cone onto the end of the spindle until it contacts the outer set of bearings. Install the washer (if equipped) and the locknut. Don't tighten the locknut yet - just turn it down until it contacts the cone or washer.

23

Adjustment

Rotate the spindle in the pedal body. It should turn freely but shouldn't feel loose. If it feels tight or loose, insert a screwdriver between the cone and the pedal body and turn the spindle one way or the other until the adjustment feels right.

Holding the pedal spindle with a wrench and using a socket, tighten the locknut securely and check the feel of the adjustment again. If it feels too tight and the pedal doesn't turn freely, loosen the locknut, insert the screwdriver between the cone and the pedal body again and turn the spindle until you feel a small amount of play, then tighten the locknut. If it feels like there is too much play, turn the spindle until the play is almost taken up, then tighten the locknut. It may take a few tries to get this adjustment right, so be patient.

Complete the procedure by installing the pedal cage and the dust cap, then mount the pedals as directed in Section 2a.

Shimano SPD type pedal overhaul

These pedals are sealed from the elements fairly well, but they are still subject to wear and, to an extent, contamination. It's wise to at least remove the spindle from the pedal every six months to check the condition of the grease in the bearings.

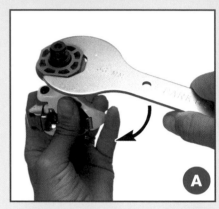

A With the pedals removed from the crank arms, hold the pedal spindle stationary with a 15 mm wrench and, using the special tool provided with your pedals, unscrew the lock bolt from the pedal body. The lock bolt on the right-side pedal has left-hand threads, so be sure to unscrew it as if you were tightening a regular fastener.

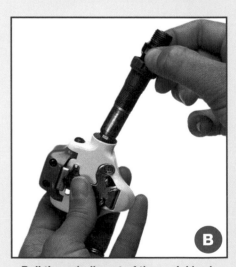

B Pull the spindle out of the pedal body and wipe it off. At this point you can adjust the bearing or continue to disassemble the spindle and clean and inspect the components.

Hold the cone with a 10 mm wrench and loosen the locknut with a 7 mm wrench. Remove the locknut.

Unscrew the cone nut, being careful not to spill the bearings. It's a good idea to work over a rag or some kind of container so if you do spill the bearings they won't go bouncing all over the place.

Remove the spacer, bearings, washer and lock bolt. There are an equal number of bearings on either side of the spacer (usually 12).

Note:

Wash all of the components with degreaser and inspect them for wear. Worn ball bearings can be replaced with bearings of the correct size, but if the cone or the spacer are worn, you'll have to replace the pedal.

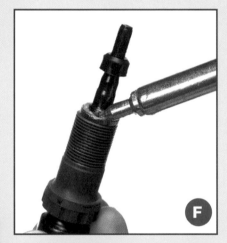

Install the lock bolt and washer onto the spindle shaft, then apply grease to the washer where the inner bearings ride.

Place half of the ball bearings into the grease on the washer.

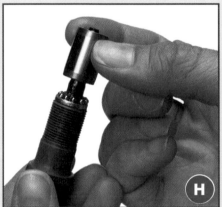

Slide the spacer onto the spindle.

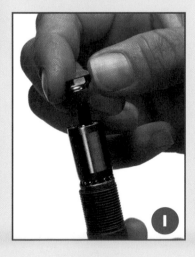

Place the remaining ball bearings on top of the spacer, then install the cone nut, threading it on until all play is taken up.

Install the locknut, threading it on until it contacts the cone. Try to move the spacer in and out and also rotate it on the spindle. If you feel any in-and-out movement, tighten the cone a little. If the spacer is hard to turn, loosen the cone until it turns freely, but with no play. When the spacer adjustment is just right, tighten the locknut against the cone, holding the cone nut with the 10 mm wrench to prevent it from tightening any more. You'll probably have to immobilize the spindle with the 15 mm wrench, since tightening the locknut may cause it to turn also. This may require the help of a friend.

Wipe out the inside of the pedal housing and insert the spindle, turning the lock bolt in the correct direction and tightening it securely.

3 Crank arms - removal and installation

If you're working on a bike with one-piece cranks, see Section 4.

Removal

1   If you're removing the right side crank arm, lift the chain off the chainwheel and rest it on the bottom bracket shell. Be sure to place a rag or tape over the bottom bracket shell so the paint won't get scratched. Also, measure the clearance between the chainstay and the closest chainring. If you're removing the crank arms to replace the bottom bracket, make sure you have the same amount of clearance (minimum 2 mm [5/64-inch]) when you reinstall the crank arm. **Photo 24**

2   Remove the dust cover, if equipped. If you see a little notch on the outside edge of the cover, insert a small screwdriver in it and pry the cover off. Plain covers must also be pried off - just be careful not to mar the cover or the crank arm in doing so. If the cover has a slot, hex or two pin hole openings in it, it must be unscrewed. Use an Allen wrench for the hex type and a small pin spanner for the pin hole type. A special tool is available for the slot type, but if you're very careful you can use a large screwdriver (some covers are made from very soft aluminum and are easily damaged). **Photo 25**

(24)

(25)

Note:

If you notice an Allen bolt head protruding through the dust cover (and the dustcap has a couple of holes in it - one on either side of the Allen-head bolt), leave the dust cover in place. This arrangement requires no special crank arm puller (skip Steps 3, 5 and 7 through 9 - read Steps 4 and 6 before reading the next sentence). Immobilize the cover with a small pin spanner and unscrew the Allen bolt - as the bolt is unscrewed (counterclockwise), it will force the crank arm off the bottom bracket spindle.

3   Remove the nut or bolt from the crank arm. Most are 14 mm, some are 15 mm or 16 mm, and some are Allen head. Whichever kind you have, unscrew it in the normal direction (counterclockwise). Check the recess in the crank arm for a washer. If present, remove it. **Photo 26**

4   Look at the crank arm-to-bottom bracket spindle relationship. If the surface on the crank arm where the nut or bolt tightens is flush with the end of the bottom bracket spindle, the crank arm is worn out and should be replaced, or is incompatible with the spindle. Either way, it won't fit on the spindle as tight as it should.

5   Check to make sure you have the proper type of crank arm puller. Most crank arms secured by nuts require one type, while most crank arms secured by bolts - Allen or hex - require another. Failure to use the right tool will result in a damaged bottom bracket spindle and/or damaged crank arms. Check with your local bike shop for advice. Some Campagnolo cranks require a puller with left-hand threads. Just be sure the end of the tool is compatible with your bottom bracket spindle and the threads on the tool are compatible with the threads in your crank arms. **Photo 27**

Note:

Some Campagnolo covers have left-hand threads and must be loosened by turning clockwise.

(26)

6   Squirt some penetrating oil onto the crank arm/bottom bracket spindle mating area. Also spray some from the back side. Let the penetrant soak in for a little while. **Photo 28**

7   Unscrew the center portion of the tool out as far as it will go, then thread the tool into the crank arm. It should turn in easy, all the way until it bottoms out (if it doesn't, stop and make sure you aren't cross-threading it).

8   Once the tool has been threaded in all the way, slightly tighten it up with a wrench.

9   Now tighten the inner part of the tool until the crank pops off the spindle. This sometimes takes a tremendous amount of effort. If possible, position the wrench so you can grasp it and the crank arm, squeezing them together. **Photo 29**

10   Lift the crank arm free, then unscrew the tool. It isn't needed for the installation procedure unless it incorporates the socket you'll need to tighten the crank arm bolt.

11   Repeat the procedure to remove the other crank arm.

Installation

12   Clean all the dirt and grime from the crank and bottom bracket spindle, then apply a thin coat of grease or anti-seize compound to the flats of the bottom bracket spindle. This will prevent the components from "freezing"

together and aid in future removal. **Photo 30**

13   Mount the crank arm onto the bottom bracket spindle and, if the other crank arm is in place, making sure it's pointing in the opposite direction (this sounds absolutely obvious, but if it's late at night and you're not paying attention . . .)

14   Apply a thin film of grease or anti-seize to the bolt threads (or, if the crank arm is retained by a nut, to the threads of the stud on the bottom bracket spindle). Install the nut or bolt and tighten it securely. **Photo 31**

15   Install the dust cover

4 Bottom bracket

4a Bearing maintenance

After hours and hours of pedaling, month after month, your bottom bracket bearings may tend to get a little sloppy. This can be verified by trying to wiggle the crank arms from side-to-side - if you feel any play (and you know the cranks are tight on the bottom bracket spindle) the bottom bracket bearings are in need of adjustment or replacement.

Some bottom brackets feature a cone-and-ball arrangement. This type can be adjusted or disassembled, cleaned and lubricated. Bikes with single-piece cranks can also be adjusted or overhauled. Many modern bottom bracket bearings are of the sealed, cartridge type. The only way to service this kind is to replace it with a new one. This section will deal with the cone-and-ball type. Refer to Part B of this Section for the cartridge-type bottom bracket replacement procedure.

4a.1 Cone-and-ball type - adjustment

1   Loosen the lockring on the left-side bearing cup of the bottom bracket. Most current designs require a lockring spanner although some older designs are hex-shaped, so a large wrench can be used. **Photo 32**

Note:

The lockring and left side bearing cup have regular right-hand threads - turn the lockring counterclockwise to loosen it.

2   Turn the bearing cup in or out, as necessary, to obtain the desired bearing adjustment. The adjustment is correct when the bottom bracket spindle turns freely but has no freeplay in it. Again, this can be checked by wiggling the crank arms from side-to-side.

a) Some cups can be turned with an open-end wrench, as shown . . . **Photo 33**

b) . . . while those that have holes in the face of the bearing cup must be turned with a pin spanner. **Photo 34**

Tip:

If you don't have a pin spanner you can engage the tips of a pair of needle-nose pliers with the holes. To do this, however, you'll first have to remove the left-side crank arm.

Bottom bracket bearing check

You can quickly determine if your bottom bracket bearings are in need of adjustment by trying to move a crank arm from side-to-side. If there is any movement, check the tightness of the crank arm fasteners - if they're tight, proceed to adjust the bottom bracket bearings. If you have a cartridge-type bottom bracket, this means you'll have to install a new one.

3   Once you've adjusted the bearing cup satisfactorily, hold it in place with the wrench or the pin spanner and tighten the lockring securely. Recheck the adjustment by wiggling the crank arms side-to-side. **Photo 35**

4a.2 Cone-and-ball type - overhaul

Disassembly

1   Remove the crank arms following the procedure described in Section 3.
2   Loosen the lockring and unscrew it completely. **Photo 36**
3   Unscrew and remove the left-side bearing cup and bearings. **Photo 37**
4   Remove the bottom bracket spindle from the bottom bracket shell. At this point, wipe all the grease from the right-side bearing cup and inspect it for pitting, flaking of the bearing surface or other signs of wear. If it's in good shape, there's no point in removing it from the frame (unless the other bearing cup is worn out, in which case you should replace the entire bottom bracket). **Photo 38**

Note:

Some bottom brackets employ a plastic dust sleeve that surrounds the spindle. If yours has this, remove it now.

5   If you are going to install a new bottom bracket, unscrew the right side bearing cup. This cup has left-hand threads, so to unscrew it you'll have to turn it clockwise. It will probably be very tight so it's best to use a tool designed for this purpose, although a large wrench could also be used (as long as the wrench fits snugly on the flats of the cup). It may be helpful to apply penetrating oil to the area where the cup and frame meet, and also to the inside of the bearing shell. You may also have to smack the wrench with a hammer to break the cup loose. **Photo 39**

4 Bottom bracket
(continued)

Inspection

6   Clean all of the components with degreaser and wipe them off with a clean rag. Inspect the bearing contact areas on the spindle and in the cups for pitting and other signs of wear. Also check the condition of the ball bearings. Replace any parts that aren't in top condition. Always take the old parts with you so you'll be sure to get the correct replacements. **Photo 40**

Tip:

Most modern cone-and-ball type bottom brackets use nine ball bearings per side, held captive in cages. There is room in most bottom bracket bearing cups for eleven bearings, but they must be put in loose (un-caged). More bearings spread the load out better (because there is more bearing contact area) so this is something you may want to think about doing. Be sure to obtain the correct size bearings. The old bearings, if they're in good shape, can simply be pried out of their cages.

Note:

If you're installing caged bearings, make sure the exposed part of the bearing faces the bearing surface in the cup.

Reassembly

7   Using a rag and degreaser, wipe the inside of the bottom bracket bearing shell clean.
8   If the right-side bearing cup was removed, apply a thick bead of grease to the inside of the cup where the bearings ride. Install the bearings into the grease (whether caged or loose) and apply a little more grease on top of them.

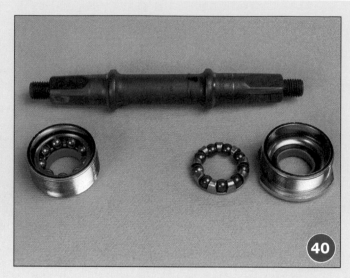

Lubricate the threads with grease or anti-seize compound and install the cup into the bottom bracket shell. Remember, it has left-hand threads, so tighten it counterclockwise. If the bearing cup uses a rubber seal around the opening, wipe some grease on it. **Photo 41**
9   Apply grease to the left-side bearing cup and install the ball bearings (read the note in the last Step). Smear a little more grease on top of the bearings. If the cup employs a rubber seal around the hole through which the spindle passes, lubricate the seal with grease. Also apply grease or anti-seize compound to the threads of the cup. If you removed a plastic dust sleeve, coat it with clean grease and install it over the spindle. **Photo 42**
10   Insert the shorter end of the bottom bracket spindle into the left bearing cup

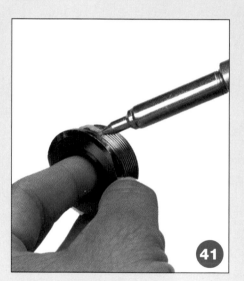

and securely hold on to the end of the spindle so the cup can't move in relation to the spindle (this will keep the bearings in place).

11 Pass the spindle through the bottom bracket bearing shell and the right side cup, taking care not to disturb the bearings. Thread the left cup into the bottom bracket shell until there is no play in the spindle. **Photo 43**

12 Install the lockring and proceed to adjust the bearing by following the procedure described in Section 4a.1.

13 Install the crank arms (see Section 3 if necessary).

4a.3 One-piece crank type - adjustment

1 Loosen the locknut by turning it clockwise. If the bearing cone turns when you do this, hold it with a bottom bracket cone spanner. **Photo 44**

2 Turn the bearing cone in or out, as necessary, to achieve the desired adjustment. The crank should be able to turn freely, but should not have any play in the bearings, either. Since the cone has left-hand threads, you'll turn it counterclockwise to tighten it. **Photo 45**

3 When you have the proper adjustment, hold the cone stationary with the cone spanner, then tighten the locknut by turning it counterclockwise. If you can't prevent the cone from turning as the locknut is tightened (which will preload the bottom bracket bearing), back the cone out a little and try tightening the locknut again. It may turn the cone along with it, but the idea is to wind up with the correct bearing adjustment when the nut is tightened fully. This could take several attempts before you get it right. **Photo 46**

4a.4 One-piece crank type - overhaul

Disassembly

1 Remove the pedals from the crank arms (see Section 2a). Detach the chain from the chainring. On multi-speed bikes simply lift the chain off the chainring(s). On single-speed bikes, loosen the rear wheel axle nuts, slide the wheel forward to produce slack in the chain, then lift the chain off the chainring.

2 Remove the locknut by unscrewing it clockwise, then slide it off the left-side crank arm. **Photo 47**

3 Unscrew the left cone by turning it clockwise.

4 Remove the left-side cone and bearing. **Photo 48**

Note:

Some cones have a hex surface for a wrench instead of the more common slotted cone shown here.

4 Bottom bracket (continued)

5 Pull the crank out the right side to dislodge the right-side bearing. Once the bearing is free of the bottom bracket the crank can be removed. **Photo 49**

6 If it is necessary to remove the right-side cone from the crank arm (because of wear [see Step 7] or if you need to replace the chainring), mount the crank in a vise lined with soft jaws and unscrew the cone. As you look at the cone from the left crank arm side, unscrew it by turning it counterclockwise. If the chainring is a one-piece type, it can be removed now, if necessary.

Inspection

7 Clean the bearings, cones, crank and bearing races with degreaser. Replace any parts that show signs of wear. If the bearing cups in the bottom bracket shell need to be replaced, take the bike to a bike shop, as these cups can be extremely difficult to remove and install. If parts need to be replaced, take the old ones with you to the bike shop so you can be sure to get the right parts. **Photo 50**

Reassembly

8 If the chainring was removed, install it on the crank arm with any identifying marks facing out. Make sure the drive hole is engaged with the drive tang on the crank.

9 Lubricate the threads of the right-side bearing cone with grease and slip it onto the crank. Thread it on in a clockwise direction as viewed from the left crank arm side and tighten it securely.

10 Lubricate the bearing cups in the frame, the bearings and the cones with grease, then install the right side bearing onto the crank, making sure it faces the proper direction. The exposed portion of the bearings must contact the cup in the frame. **Photo 51**

11 Insert the crank through the bottom bracket shell. Pass the left bearing over the left crank arm and slide it into position, making sure you put it on with the exposed portion of the bearings facing the bearing cup in the frame. **Photo 52**

12 Install the left bearing cone, threading it on in a counterclockwise

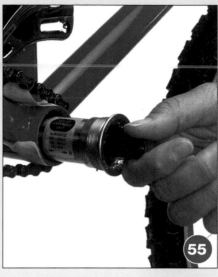

direction. Tighten it just enough to re-move all play in the bottom bracket bearings. **Photo 53**

13 Install the locknut, but don't tighten it until the bottom bracket bearings have been adjusted as de-scribed in Section 4a.3.

14 Install the pedals (see Section 2) and the chain. if you're working on a single-speed bike adjust the chain so you have about 1/2-inch of slack in the center of the chain run.

4b Cartridge-type bottom bracket - replacement

The only reason you would have to replace a cartridge-type bottom bracket is if it has developed freeplay in the bearings or suffers from rough, gritty operation. To perform this pro-cedure you'll need a special tool to re-move the spline-drive bottom bracket "cups."

1 Remove the crank arms from the bottom bracket spindle (see Sec-tion 3).

2 Look at each side of the bottom bracket. One side will have a recessed cup (the support cup) that fits entirely into the bottom bracket shell, while the other side has a flange that bears against the side of the bottom bracket shell. On some cartridges the support

cup is on the right side of the bike - on others it's on the left. Using the special tool, unscrew the support cup (which is really no more than a collar) from the bottom bracket shell. Whichever type you are removing, just remember that the right side portion of the assembly, be it the support cup or the cartridge assembly, has left-hand threads and

Note:

Some sealed cartridge-type bottom brackets are held in place by two lockrings and are adjustable from side-to-side. This allows the chainline (the alignment of the chain from the chainrings to the rear sprockets) to be adjusted slightly. Some sealed cartridge bottom brackets are pressed into the bottom bracket shell and retained by snap-rings. These two types of bottom brackets are fairly uncommon and won't be specifically dealt with here. Lockring removal for the lockring type is similar to that of the cone-and-ball type.

unscrews in the clockwise direction. The left side unscrews in the counter-clockwise direction. **Photo 54**

3 Now unscrew the cartridge as-sembly from the bottom bracket shell using the special tool. Take the as-sembly with you to the bike shop so you're sure to get the proper replace-ment parts. **Photo 55**

4 Clean the bottom bracket shell, making sure there is no foreign mater-ial on the threads.

5 Begin installing the new assembly by lubricating the support cup threads with grease and threading the support cup part-way into the bottom bracket bearing shell. **Photo 56** Remember, the threads on the right side of the shell are left-handed (backwards); the threads on the left side of the shell are right-handed (regular). Make sure the support cup goes into the same side of the bearing shell as it was removed from.

Tip:

If you're installing a titanium bottom bracket, coat the threads with anti-seize compound.

4 Bottom bracket
(continued)

6   Lubricate the threads of the bottom bracket cartridge and install it into the bottom bracket shell, being careful not to cross-thread it. Thread the unit into the bottom bracket shell until the flange contacts the shell face, then

tighten it down securely. **Photo 57**

7   Now go to the other side and tighten the support cup until it bottoms out. there's no need to get it really tight - just secure.

8   Install the crank arms and engage the chain with the chainring.

6

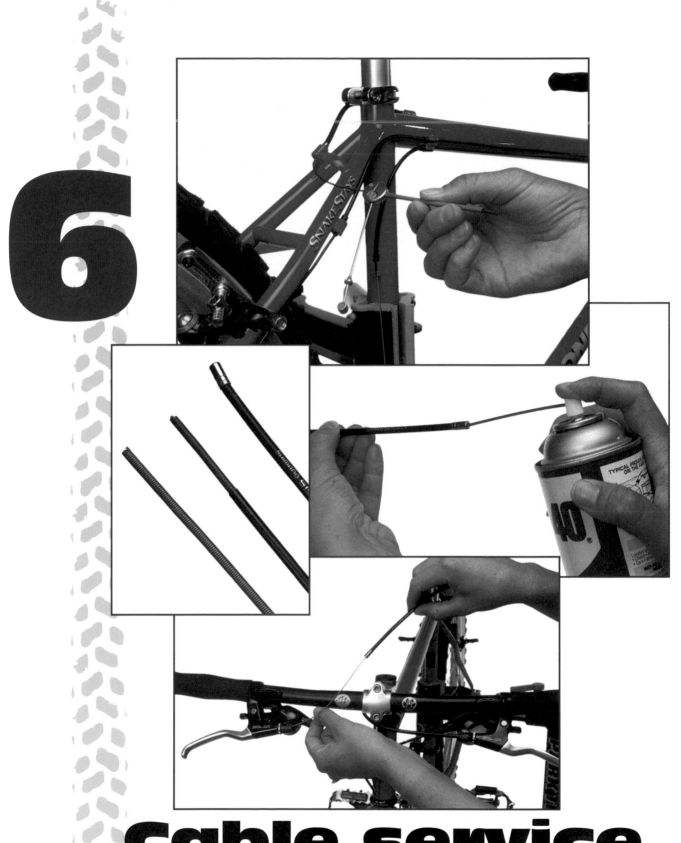

cable service

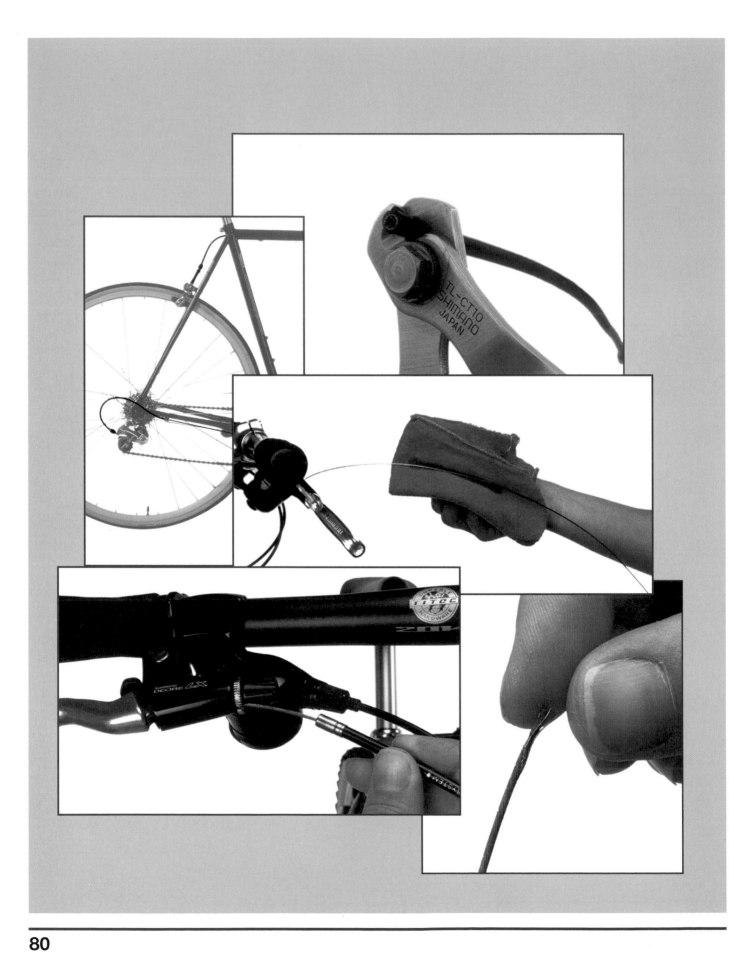

6 Cable service

Contents

Introduction

Control cables are rarely given much thought - not until they get kinked, break or bind-up with rust, that is. The first sign of a cable problem is an increased amount of effort required to operate a brake lever or a shifter. As time passes, this condition can advance and cause the brake to not release fully or not allow the derailleur to shift to the smaller sprockets or chainrings. Eventually it will break or you'll just get so tired of the sluggish operation of the cable-controlled component that you'll service or replace the cable.

1 Cable types

Cables come in a variety of diameters and types of construction. Inner shift cable thicknesses range from 1.2 mm to 1.6 mm; brake cable inners vary from 1.6 mm to 2 mm, typically. Some are made of braided steel strands, while some are smooth, spiral wound. Cable ends could either be disc, barrel or mushroom type. Cable casings differ, too - there are casings made of round-wound wire, flat-wound wire and, on most index shifter systems, casings composed of longitudinally wrapped wire strands (these are necessary because of their high resistance to compression). These are usually labeled "Shimano SP" or simply "SP." Casings can either be lined with plastic or unlined. **Photos 1 and 2**

The important thing to remember when purchasing replacement cable is to take the old cable with you to the bike shop so you can be sure to obtain the correct replacement part. Many bike shops carry universal inner cables that have a disc-type end on one end and a barrel-type end on the other end. All you have to do is cut off the end which you don't need.

When replacing a shift cable casing it's a good idea to install a Shimano SP cable casing regardless of what type of shifters you have on your bike. This type of cable will improve the performance of all shifting systems because of its rigidity.

Tip:

If you go to the bike shop to purchase a new cable casing, you may be forced to by a length that is much too long for your needs. Ask the people at the shop if they can cut a piece of casing from a bulk roll to your required length.

Tools you may need

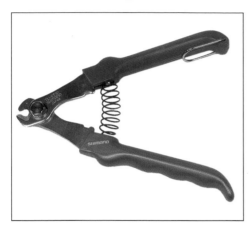

You'll need some type of cable cutter if you plan on replacing cables. This Shimano tool cuts cable casings as well as inner cables, and has an area behind the pivot point for reshaping the stranded SP cable used in SIS shifting systems. The only drawback to this tool is its price

This Park cable cutter only cuts inner cables, but it's much more economical than the Shimano tool. Inner cables are replaced much more frequently than cable casings, so this tool is probably the type you should opt for

A small nail is a good tool for opening up the plastic liner after cutting a cable casing (not all casings have plastic liners)

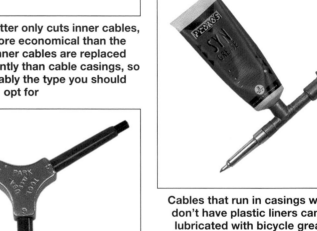

Cables that run in casings which don't have plastic liners can be lubricated with bicycle grease

Degreaser can be used for cleaning inner cables thoroughly

You may need an Allen wrench to unscrew cable clamp bolts

A lightweight penetrating oil is good for cable lubrication and for rinsing out dirty cable casings

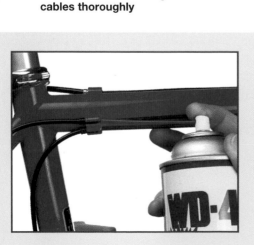

Quick lube

Between major cable servicing or after washing your bike, shoot a little penetrating oil where the cables enter their casings. This will help to keep your braking and shifting systems working smoothly.

Troubleshooting

Problem	Possible cause	Remedy
Hard to shift gears (front or rear)	Shift cable dry or worn	Lubricate or replace shift cable
Delayed shifts (front or rear)	Shift cable dry, rusty or worn	Clean and lubricate or replace cable
Rear derailleur won't shift chain to biggest sprocket (lowest gear)	Rear derailleur shift cable out of adjustment, sticky or worn Rear derailleur stop screw out of adjustment	Adjust, lubricate or replace rear derailleur shift cable Adjust derailleur (see Chapter 7)
Rear derailleur won't shift chain to smallest sprocket (highest gear)	Rear derailleur shift cable out of adjustment, sticky or worn Rear derailleur stop screw out of adjustment	Adjust, lubricate or replace rear derailleur shift cable Adjust derailleur (see Chapter 7)
Rear derailleur does not shift accurately	Rear derailleur shift cable sticky or worn	Lubricate or replace rear derailleur shift cable
Front derailleur won't shift chain to biggest chainring	Front derailleur shift cable out of adjustment or sticky Front derailleur stop screw out of adjustment	Adjust, lubricate or replace front derailleur shift cable Adjust derailleur (see Chapter 7)
Front derailleur won't shift chain to smallest chainring	Front derailleur shift cable out of adjustment, worn or sticky Front derailleur stop screw out of adjustment	Adjust, lubricate or replace front derailleur shift cable Adjust derailleur (see Chapter 7)
Front derailleur shifting not precise or is inconsistent	Front derailleur shift cable sticky or worn	Lubricate or replace cable
Brake pad(s) rub on rim	Brake not returning fully due to sticky cable Brake out of adjustment	Clean and lubricate or replace cable Adjust brake (see Chapter 9)
Brake lever(s) hard to pull	Brake cable(s) dry Brake cable(s) and/or casing(s) worn	Lubricate cable(s) Replace cable(s)

2 Cable lubrication

Occasionally (every six months or so) your cables should be given a more thorough lubrication than the simple squirt of WD40 that you apply after cleaning your bike. This lubrication process requires the withdrawal of the inner cable from the casing, giving you a chance to inspect the entire length of cable for damage and wear. This routine lubrication will prevent the formation of rust and prolong cable life, making your bike safer and more enjoyable to ride.

Refer to Chapter 7 or Chapter 9 and detach the cable from the derailleur or the brake. Trim off any frayed cable ends (this will make reassembly easier). If the cable is frayed all the way up to the clamp bolt on the derailleur or brake, think seriously about replacing the inner cable with a new one.

Slide the cable casing off the inner cable. On some cables it's easier to pull the inner cable out, leaving the casing undisturbed (where casings run under handlebar tape, for example). Refer to Section 3 for inner cable removal details.

Spray penetrating oil (WD40 or equivalent) into the cable casing to flush it out and lubricate it.

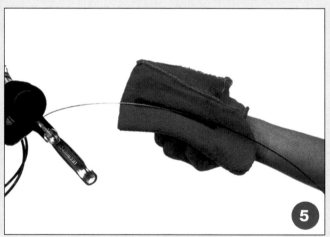

Clean the inner cable with a rag soaked in degreaser or solvent to remove all rust and grime.

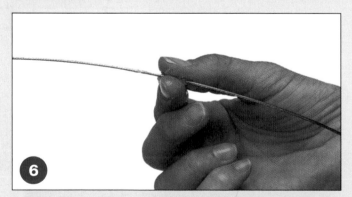

Rub grease onto the inner cable in the areas where the cable rides in the casing. Slide the casing back onto the inner cable, making sure you route the inner through any guides in the frame that are present along its run (see Section 3). Connect the cable to the derailleur or brake and adjust it (see Chapter 7 or 9).

Note:

If the cable casing has a liner, don't apply grease - WD40 or equivalent, or preferably a dry lube, should be used.

Related lubrication points

In addition to lubricating your cables, be sure to periodically lubricate the pivot points at the brake levers, brake arms and derailleurs.

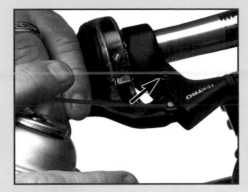

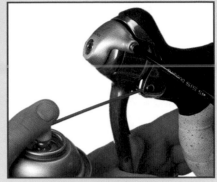

3 Cable replacement

3a Shift cable

If your bike is equipped with GripShift type shifters, refer to the sidebar which follows this procedure.

1   If you're replacing a rear shift cable on an STI or Rapidfire-type index shift system, shift the rear derailleur into high gear (the smallest sprocket). If you're replacing the front cable, shift the chain onto the smallest chainring. If the cable is broken and this can't be done, grab an exposed portion of the inner cable that's still connected to the shifter and pull on it firmly while operating the upshift lever (rear) or down-shift lever (front) repeatedly (you'll feel the cable "give" or lengthen each time you actuate the shifter). This will place the shift ratchet mechanism in the re-

laxed position so the cable can be removed.

2   Loosen the clamp bolt and detach the inner cable from the derailleur (see Chapter 7).

3   If you're replacing the cable casing near the derailleur, pull the casing off the inner cable (the casing at the rear derailleur is a common victim of crashes). If this is the only portion of cable you intend to replace, slide the

Note:

If the cable has broken off inside the shift mechanism, you might have to take the bike to a bike shop if you can't return the mechanism to the relaxed position.

new one on and adjust the rear derailleur (see Chapter 7).

4   Lift the cable out of its slot in the casing stop on the frame. Remove the cable sheath (the thin covering over inner cables that don't run in casings), if equipped. **Photo 7**

3 Cable replacement
(continued)

5   Push on the inner cable to feed it through the small hole in the shift lever, then pull the cable free. As stated in Step 1, the shift mechanism must be in the relaxed position.

Photo 8 shows a mountain bike with early Shimano Rapidfire shifters (on some models you'll have to remove the plastic cover for access).

Photo 9 shows a mountain bike with Shimano Rapidfire Plus shifters (on this type, you may first have to remove a small rubber plug from the hole before the cable will come out).

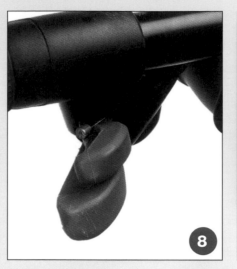

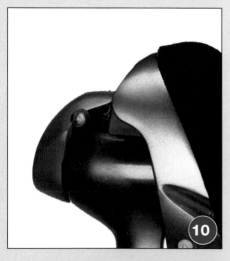

Photo 10 shows a road bike with Shimano STI shifters (pull the brake lever in to expose the hole for the shift cable).

6   If you're also replacing the cable casing on a road bike with shift cables concealed under the handlebar tape, Remove the tape following the procedure described in Chapter 11.

7   Detach the cable casing from the shifter.

8   If necessary, cut your cable casing(s) to the proper length and finish off the ends so there aren't any burrs (see Section 4).

9   Install the new cable and casing by reversing the removal procedure, but keep these points in mind:

a) Lubricate the cable as described in Section 2.

b) Make sure the cable is routed properly, with no sharp bends.

c) If the cable is routed under the bottom bracket, make sure it is seated in the groove in the cable guide. **Photo 11**

d) Always install ferrules onto the cable ends where they contact cable casing stops.

e) Don't forget to adjust the derailleurs (see Chapter 7).

f) Install cable end caps onto the ends of all bare cables to prevent fraying (and to keep from getting poked by an errant strand of wire!).

GripShift cable replacement

On some types of GripShift shifters a small Phillips head screw on the side of the shifter housing can be unscrewed and a plate removed, giving you access to the cable (which can be pulled through after detaching it from the derailleur). On models without this screw and plate this becomes a job best left to a bike shop. Routing the cable into and out of the shifter is not all that difficult, but separating the shifter ring from the housing can be somewhat tricky, and if not performed just right it's easy to break the little tab that holds the two parts together. There's also a detent spring inside that usually falls out when the shifter ring is separated from the housing.

The bike shop probably won't charge much to replace the cable (especially if you purchased the bike from them) and, if they mess up your shifter they'll be the ones liable for replacing it!

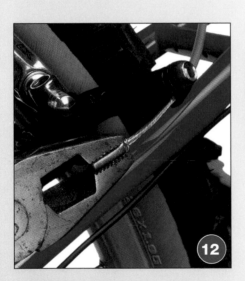

3b Brake cable

1   Pull the cable end off the cable, if one is present. **Photo 12**

2   Free the end of the cable from the brake. This is accomplished by loosening the clamp bolt from the:

a) brake arm on side-pull brakes. **Photo 13**

b) brake arm on link-wire cantilever brakes, then slide the cable through the sheath and out of the cable hanger. **Photo 14**

c) yoke on straddle wire cantilever, center-pull and U-brakes (this will require two wrenches - one for the bolt and one for the nut on the other side. **Photo 15**

Tip:
If the cable is going to be replaced with a new one and the cable end is frayed, go ahead and cut the frayed part of the cable off.

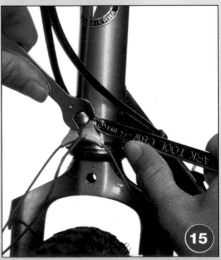

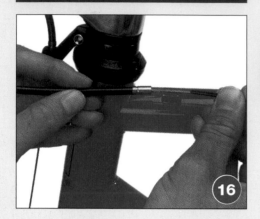
16

17

18

19

20

3   If the cable casing doesn't run under the handlebar tape, detach the cable and casing from any cable stops on the frame. **Photo 16**

4   Road bikes: Pull the brake lever in completely, push the cable up through the lever and remove it. If you have Shimano STI shift levers you may have to angle the lever toward the center of the bike as you pull it in to provide adequate clearance. **Photo 17**

5   Mountain bikes (and hybrids and BMX bikes):

a) Align the slots in the cable adjuster and the locknut and lever mount. Pull the casing back and pass the inner cable through the slot. **Photo 18**

b) Pull the brake lever in, pass the cable through the slot in the underside of the lever and free the cable end. Remove the cable from the casing. **Photo 19**

> ### Note:
> *If there's no slot in the lever mount, detach the cable end from the lever and unscrew the adjuster from the mount, pulling the cable free.*

6   If necessary, remove the handlebar tape (see Chapter 11) and replace the cable casing.

7   If it's too long, cut your cable casing to the proper length and finish off the ends so there aren't any burrs (see Section 4).

8   Install the new cable and casing by reversing the removal procedure, but keep these points in mind:

a) Lubricate the cable as described in Section 2.

b) Make sure the cable is routed properly, with no sharp bends.

c) On road bikes with STI levers, be sure the cable guide (the piece that fits over the casing from the lever mount and around the first bend of the handlebar) is fully engaged with the lever mount. This can be confirmed by peeling the rubber cover back and looking through the hole in the side of the mount. Tape this cable guide into place along the leading edge of the handlebar. **Photo 20**

d) Always install ferrules onto the casing ends where they contact casing stops on the frame.

e) Don't forget to adjust the brakes (see Chapter 9).

f) Crimp cable end caps onto the ends of all bare cables to prevent fraying (and to prevent the cable from taking an unwanted blood sample).

4 Cutting cables and casings

Improperly cut cables and casings will give a bike that "unfinished" look and feel. Inner cables that aren't cut neatly and capped are destined to fray, making them very difficult to deal with when it comes time to service them. They can also stick you, which will induce about as much euphoria as a paper cut.

Cable casings that aren't cut properly will cause a "spongy" feel to the brakes (kind of like air in an automotive braking system). Shifting, especially if your bike is equipped with index shifters, will become inaccurate and inconsistent. Ragged casing cuts can also cause inner cables to fail. Whenever trimming cables, take the time to do it right - you'll notice the difference.

Most cable casings also can be cut with regular cutting pliers, but the damage that is inflicted is more obvious and takes more time to correct.

Cable casings should be cut short enough so there isn't lots of excess cable dangling around, but never so

4a Inner cables

21

Inner cables may be cut with a pair of diagonal cutting pliers, but this practice can distort the cable end, smashing it and causing it to fray. If you plan on doing much bicycle repair, get a pair of proper cable cutters.

short that a bend becomes too abrupt or restricts the steering movement or operation of a brake or derailleur.

Always install a ferrule onto a cable casing wherever it contacts a cable stop on the frame, or where the casing meets a brake or shift lever mount. It isn't always necessary to install a ferrule onto the casing where it enters a side-pull brake arm or some cable

22

After cutting an inner cable, twist any stray wire strands back into the cable. If some strands just won't seat, the end of the wire can be soldered and filed so it will pass through a casing without getting jammed. After the cable has been installed in the casing, connected to its component and adjusted, install a cable end and crimp it in place.

hangers. This really depends on the fit of the cable in the arm or hanger; if it is a snug fit, and the surface where the casing seats is flat (not conical), it doesn't need a ferrule.

4b Cable casings

23

When cutting cable casings, it's best to use a tool specifically for this purpose, but diagonal cutting pliers will work (except on SP cable). If you're cutting a round-wound or flat-wound cable, slice the outer covering with a razor blade, place the cable in the jaws of the tool and bend it sharply so the jaws of the cutting tool separate the windings of the cable, then cut. Proceed to clean up the cut area.

24

File or grind the end of the casing so the cut is absolutely flat (perpendicular to the length of the casing). If you choose to take the casing to a grinder, only take off a little material at a time, allowing the casing to cool off so it won't lose its temper and become too flexible. It may also be necessary to insert a small finishing nail into the end to spread it open a little.

When cutting Shimano SP shift cables, keep the cable straight while cutting.

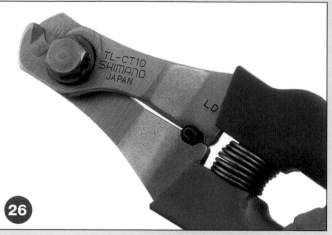

After the cut has been made, reshape the casing with the half-round jaw portion of the cutting tool. This will restore the cable opening, aligning the strands and making it round once again.

To install a ferrule, push it onto the casing as far as you can, then tap the casing and ferrule onto a hard surface to drive it on fully. If it's a loose fit, lightly crimp it in place.

7

Shifters and derailleurs

Shifters and derailleurs

Contents

Introduction

Shifters and derailleurs work in conjunction with each other, via the control cables, to move the derailleurs in and out to change gear ratios. This setup makes for a fairly trouble-free shifting system, reducing most servicing to simple lubrication and adjustment from time to time. After many hours of use, though, accumulations of grime on the sprockets and derailleurs must be removed or performance will suffer.

At first glance, the shifting system on a modern, multi-speed bike may seem a bit too complex to service yourself. Once you understand how the system works, however, you'll realize that it is really quite straightforward.

Troubleshooting

Problem	Possible cause	Remedy
Hard to shift gears (front or rear)	Derailleur dirty or worn	Clean or replace derailleur
Derailleur slips out of gear (front or rear)	Index shifters - shifter detents worn out	Replace shifter
	Non-index shifters - shifter tension screw loose or friction washers worn out	Tighten tension screw or replace friction washers
Delayed shifts (front or rear)	Derailleur sticky or worn	Clean and lubricate or replace derailleur
Chain "clatters" on sprockets	Rear derailleur shift indexing out of adjustment	Adjust rear derailleur shift cable
	Rear derailleur guide pulley worn out	Replace guide pulley
Chain falls off sprockets while shifting	Rear derailleur stop screws out of adjustment	If the chain falls off into the spokes, adjust the "L" stop screw. If the chain falls off between sprocket and frame, adjust the "H" stop screw
Rear derailleur won't shift chain to biggest sprocket (lowest gear)	Rear derailleur stop screw misadjusted	Adjust "L" stop screw on rear derailleur
Rear derailleur won't shift chain to smallest sprocket (highest gear)	Rear derailleur stop screw misadjusted	Adjust "H" stop screw on rear derailleur
	Rear derailleur return spring weak	Rear derailleur return spring weak
	Rear derailleur extremely dirty	Clean and lubricate rear derailleur
	Shift cable dry or worn	Lubricate or replace shift cable (see Chapter 6)
Rear derailleur does not shift accurately	Rear derailleur indexing out of adjustment	Adjust rear derailleur shift cable
	Rear derailleur worn out	Replace rear derailleur
Front derailleur won't shift chain to biggest chainring	Front derailleur stop screw misadjusted	Adjust outer (H) stop screw
Front derailleur won't shift chain to smallest chainring	Front derailleur stop screw misadjusted	Adjust inner (L) stop screw
	Front derailleur return spring weak	Replace spring or front derailleur
	Front derailleur cage bent or spread open	Straighten cage or replace derailleur
	Front derailleur extremely dirty	Clean and lubricate front derailleur
	Shift cable dry or worn	Lubricate or replace shift cable (see Chapter 6)
Front derailleur shifting not precise or is inconsistent	Front derailleur not positioned properly	Move derailleur down into proper position, or adjust until derailleur cage plates are parallel with the chainrings
	Derailleur inner plate excessively worn	Replace derailleur

Shifters and derailleurs

Problem	Possible cause	Remedy
Chainring rubs against front derailleur	Front derailleur out of adjustment	Adjust front derailleur
Front derailleur rubs on chain in more than one chainring	Front derailleur crooked	Adjust front derailleur parallel with chainrings
Front derailleur rubs on chain in middle or big chainring	Shifter indexing out of adjustment	Adjust front derailleur shift cable tension

Tools you may need

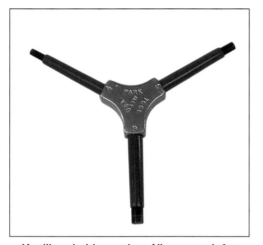

You'll probably need an Allen wrench for loosening the cable clamp bolts on the derailleurs

A cable puller, also known as a "Fourth hand" tool, is helpful for taking the slack out of shift cables

A lightweight penetrating oil such as WD40 should be used for lubricating the derailleur pivot points and shift cables

You'll need a cable cutter for trimming inner cables to length when replacing them

If you're going to replace a cable casing, you'll need a cutter like this capable of handling the job. This one's designed to cut the stranded SP casing used in SIS index shifting systems

1 Shifters

There are many different types of shifters, but they all do the same thing - they pull the control cable to move the derailleur towards a larger diameter sprocket or chainring, or loosen the cable to allow the derailleur (which is under spring tension) to move back towards a smaller diameter sprocket or chainring. This action places the chain onto the desired sprocket to obtain the gear ratio required for the current riding condition.

Early shifting systems rely on the rider to find the correct position of the shifter after the shift is made, so the chain is centered on the sprocket or chainring. This is done by listening for the clattering of the chain against another sprocket (rear) or the derailleur cage (front) and moving the lever as necessary to eliminate the noise.

Late model shifting systems employ indexed shifters which move the derailleur a predetermined amount per shift, taking care of the shift and aligning the derailleur with the sprocket or chainring at the same time. This system is much faster and, when adjusted properly, much more accurate. The shifting principle is still the same - the shifter pulls a cable to move the derailleur towards a larger diameter sprocket or chainring and loosens the cable via a ratcheting mechanism to allow the derailleur to move towards a smaller diameter sprocket or chainring, one sprocket or chainring per click of the shifter.

Stem mounted

Down tube mounted

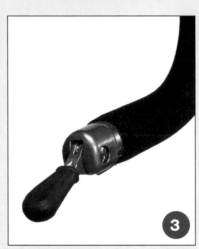

Handlebar end mounted

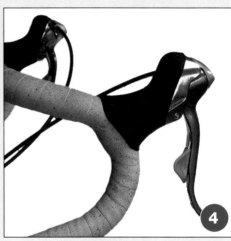

Brake lever mounted

1a Shifter types

Many different shifters and mounting arrangements have been used over the years. The following are examples of the most common types:

1   **Stem mounted** - Some older, mostly lower-end ten-speeds were equipped with these. They work fine (for a non-index type shifter), but can easily be knocked into another gear by the rider's knees. The wing nut, D-ring or screw secures the lever and can be tightened if the lever slips. **Photo 1**

2   **Down tube mounted** - This is probably the most popular shifter for road bikes. Earlier models with non-index shifting like this one use friction washers under the levers to resist the spring tension of the derailleur. The wing nut, D-ring or screw secures the lever and can be tightened if the lever slips. Recent road bikes with down tube shifters are equipped with indexed shifting systems. The D-ring on these can be turned one way for index shifting and to another position for non-index shifting (this is handy if the index shifting function loses its adjustment while you're on a ride, or if you're riding up steep inclines and can't afford to let up on the pedals much while downshifting). **Photo 2**

3   **Handlebar end mounted** - These slip into the end of the handlebar and fasten in place by an expanding collar. The cable is routed under the handlebar tape. Early models are friction (non-

index) type levers, later systems are indexed. **Photo 3**

4 **Brake lever mounted** - These Shimano STI (stands for Shimano Total Integration) levers incorporate the shifters into the brake levers. Shifting is accomplished by pushing the levers inwards. When the entire lever is pushed, the derailleur moves the chain to the next larger sprocket or chainring. When the small lever on the backside of the main lever is pushed, the ratchet inside the lever mechanism is released one pawl (or notch), allowing the derailleur to bring the chain onto the next smaller sprocket or chainring. Very slick, since it allows shifting without removing your hands from the handlebars. **Photo 4**

5 **Thumb shifters** - Found on mountain bikes and hybrids, these shifters are actuated by your thumbs and index fingers. They are convenient and very reliable.

Photo 5 shows a thumb shifter on a vintage mountain bike with non-index shifting. Like a down tube mounted shifter on a road bike, the D-ring on top of the shifter may have to be tightened occasionally to prevent the derailleur from jumping into another gear.

Photo 6 shows a thumb shifter on an early index shifting system. The kind shown in the accompanying photo has a small lever that can be set in the index position (SIS) or the friction position (F). The friction position is a real benefit if the index mechanism in the shifter lets go while you're on a ride.

6 **Rapidfire shifters** - Brought on the scene by Shimano, these shifters

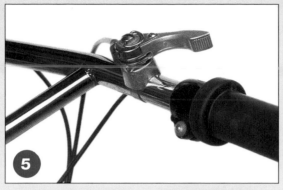

Thumb shifter - friction type

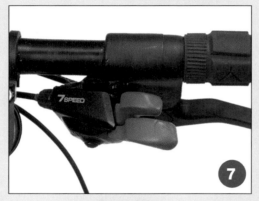

Rapidfire

Thumb shifter - index type

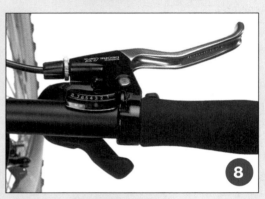

Rapidfire Plus

GripShift

give the rider full command of the gears without removing his or her hands from the grips.

a) The early versions of Rapidfire systems are sometimes referred to as "push-push" shifters, because one button is pushed for upshifts and another is pushed for downshifts. **Photo 7**

b) Later versions, called Rapidfire Plus, were redesigned to be actuated by thumb and index finger (like a trigger). The thumb lever moves the derailleur towards a larger diameter sprocket or chainring. The finger trigger allows the derailleur to move towards the next smaller diameter sprocket or chainring, one position per pull. **Photo 8**

7 **GripShift** - This type of index shifter is actuated by twisting a collar

which forms the inner portion of the hand grip, allowing the rider to shift without removing any fingers from the grip. Twisting the grip one click towards you (like opening the throttle on a motorcycle) moves the derailleur towards the next larger diameter sprocket or chainring. A version is also available for road bikes which mounts the twist shifter on the ends of the drops. **Photo 9**

1b Removal and installation

1b.1 Stem mounted shifters

Levers

If you plan on replacing the lever (due to damage) or removing it completely, begin by removing the shift cable.

Lever mounts

Some stem-mounted shifters are secured to the stem by a clamp. Remove the stem (see Chapter 11 if necessary), loosen the clamp screw, separate the clamp and detach the assembly from the stem. Install the mount by reversing the removal procedure, taking care to line-up the mount with the handlebar.

If you're just removing the lever for service, loosen the D-ring, wing nut or screw and remove the outer plate and/or washer.

Slide the lever off the mounting boss or screw. Note the locations of all washers and spacers. Some have thin friction washers that should be cleaned, but not lubed. Similarly, some have nylon washers which don't require lubrication. Apply a light film of grease to all metal-on-metal surfaces.

Other stem-mounts are secured by the upper headset locknut. To remove it, remove the stem (see Chapter 11), unscrew the locknut and lift the mount off the steerer tube. Installation is the reverse of removal.

1b.2 Down tube mounted shifters

Levers

If you plan on replacing the lever (due to damage) or removing it completely, begin by removing the shift cable.

Note the locations of all washers and spacers. Some have thin friction washers that should be cleaned, but not lubed. Similarly, some have nylon washers which don't require lubrication. Apply a light film of grease to all metal-on-metal surfaces.

If you're just removing the lever for service, loosen the D-ring, wing nut or screw and remove the outer plate and/or washer.

Slide the lever off the mounting boss or screw.

Lever mounts

Many down tube mounted shifters are attached to brazed-on bosses. Others are secured to removable clamps.

When installing, position the mount against the locating lug or the piece of tape, align the mount so the centerline of the lever pivot screws are parallel to the ground, then install the clamp bolt and tighten it securely. Install the shift levers.

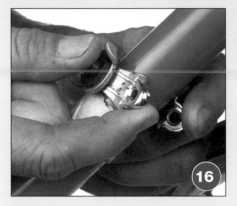

To remove the clamp, first take off the shift levers. Mark the position of the clamp with a piece of tape (if there's no lug below the mount), unscrew the clamp bolt and carefully spread the mount apart just enough to detach it from the frame. Be careful not to scratch the paint.

1b.3 Handlebar end mounted shifters

Shift the derailleur onto the largest sprocket or chainring, then without pedaling, move the shift lever the other way. This should provide enough slack in the cable to allow lever removal. Now refer to photos 17 and 18 and perform the steps described in the captions.

During installation, apply a film of grease to the expansion screw threads. Install the lever body into the end of the handlebar, making sure the opening slot for the lever is perpendicular to the ground. Turn the expansion screw counterclockwise until the body is secure.

Lubricate the pivot and the thin washers on the lever with a light film of grease, install the lever in the body and insert the pivot. You'll probably have to line up the flats in the small washers with the flats on the pivot. Install the pivot screw and tighten it enough to provide a fair amount of drag when the lever is moved (you can tighten it up later, if necessary). Install the locknut, if equipped.

Remove the screw and pivot from the lever body (some designs have a locknut on the other end of the screw which should be removed first). It'll probably be necessary to back the screw out a few turns then tap it with a soft-face hammer to dislodge the lever pivot from the housing.

Pull the lever and cable out far enough to allow a wrench to be inserted into the lever body. Be careful not to lose the thin washers on either side of the lever. Insert an Allen wrench (usually 6 mm) into the lever body expansion screw and turn it clockwise to decrease the diameter of the internal clamp. The lever body can now be withdrawn from the bar.

1b.4 Brake lever mounted (STI) shifters

Note: *The following procedure shouldn't be performed unless the shift/brake lever absolutely must be removed (for replacement after an accident, for example).*

Shift the derailleur until the chain is on the smallest sprocket or chainring. This will place the index ratcheting mechanism within the shifter in the relaxed position. Loosen the cable clamp at the derailleur, remove the cable end and remove the shift cable, pulling it through the hole in the shift lever (see Chapter 6).

Loosen the brake cable clamp on the brake controlled by the lever you're removing. This will give you the slack you'll need to detach the lever from the cable "hook" or "barrel." Refer to photos 19 through 22 and perform the steps described in the captions.

The lever can be separated from the index unit, but lever replacement really is a job that should be performed by a bike shop mechanic. At least you'll save the labor cost of removing and installing the lever from the mount, and you won't have to haul your entire bike to the shop.

Installing the lever is the reverse of the removal procedure, with the following points:
a) Make sure the washers and bushings are properly situated on the brake cable hook.
b) Make sure the bent end of the

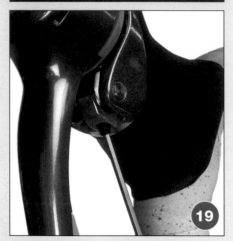

19

Unscrew the small set screw from the underside of the lever mount.

spring is installed in the hole in the lever, and the bushings are in place (the spring should surround the longer bushing).

c) Be sure to tighten the pivot stud set screw securely.

Make sure the spring surrounds the longer bushing, and the end of the spring is in the hole.

20

Drive out the lever pivot stud with a narrow punch and a hammer.

22

21

Gently pull the lever out of the mount and detach the brake cable "hook" or "barrel" from the U-shaped cutouts on the back of the lever.

Caution:
Note the locations of the lever pivot bushings and the return spring, as well as the bushings and washers on the brake cable hook. These are very small parts and will probably fall out when the lever is removed.

1b.5 Thumb shifters (above bar)

Remove the grip from the handlebar, followed by the brake lever (see Chapters 11 and 9, respectively).

Tip
If you're removing the shifter to replace the handlebar, you may be able to leave the cable attached if the cable casing is long enough to allow the shifter to be slid off the end of the handlebar. If not, or if you're removing the shifter because of damage, detach the shift cable from the derailleur and pull it through the hole in the shifter.

23

On early model thumb shifters, unscrew the wing nut or D-ring screw from the top of the lever and separate the lever from the mount.

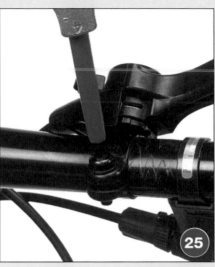

To remove the mount, loosen the nut a couple of turns and slide the mount off the handlebar.

On later model thumb shifters, loosen the shifter clamp bolt and slide the shifter off the handlebar.

Tip:
If you're removing the shifter to replace the handlebar, you may be able to leave the cable attached if the cable casing is long enough to allow the shifter to be slid off the end of the handlebar. If not, or if you're removing the shifter because of damage, detach the shift cable from the derailleur and pull it through the hole in the shifter.

1b.6 Shimano Rapidfire and Rapidfire Plus type shifters

1b.6a Rapidfire (early type)

Remove the grip from the handlebar, followed by the brake lever (see Chapters 11 and 9, respectively).

Loosen the clamp bolt and slide the shifter off the handlebar (early Rapidfire shifter shown).

1b.6b Rapidfire Plus (later type)

This type of shifter is integral with the brake lever. Refer to Chapter 9 for the brake lever removal procedure.

1b.7 GripShift shifters

Remove the grip from the handlebar (see Chapter 11 if necessary). Take off the thin washer between the grip and the shifter.

If it is necessary to completely remove the shifter and cable from the bike, detach the cable at the derailleur and pull the inner cable out of its housing. It isn't a good idea to disassemble the shifter and remove the inner cable - leave that job for a bike shop (see the sidebar in Chapter 6).

Installation is the reverse of removal. Be sure to tighten the set screw securely, and make sure the shifter does not interfere with the brake lever (if it does, reposition it).

Loosen the set screw on the shifter housing and slide the shifter off the handlebar.

2 Derailleurs

Derailleurs all function in the same manner. When a rider downshifts the rear derailleur, for example, the derailleur pushes the chain towards the next larger diameter sprocket. As the chain begins to rub against the sprocket, the teeth on the sprocket engage the side plates on the chain, lifting the chain up onto the sprocket. When it's time for an upshift, the derailleur pulls the chain towards the next smaller diameter sprocket, causing the chain to climb up over the teeth on the sprocket and drop down to the smaller one.

Index shifting systems also work like this, but the "throw" of the shifter (the amount it pulls or releases the shift cable) is calibrated to move the derailleur the exact amount to execute the shift.

2a Removal and installation

2a.1 Front derailleur

Removal

Front derailleur

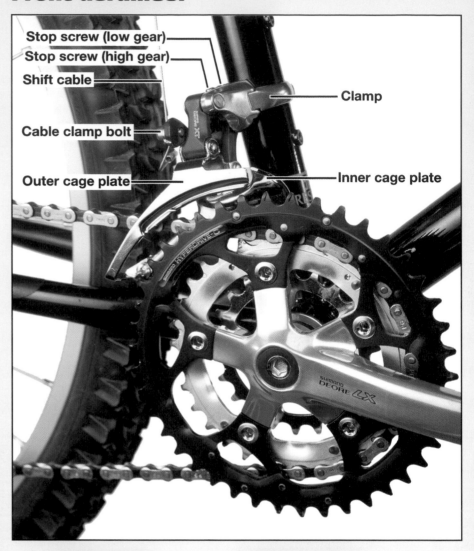

Stop screw (low gear)
Stop screw (high gear)
Shift cable
Cable clamp bolt
Outer cage plate
Clamp
Inner cage plate

28

If possible, shift the chain onto the smallest chainring, then remove the screw from the rear of the cage plates and take out the spacer.

Note:
On some models you'll have to do this after the derailleur has been removed from the frame.

29

Loosen the cable clamp bolt and free the cable from the clamp.

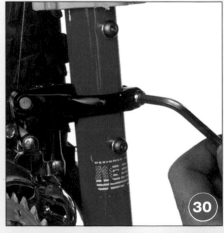

30

Unscrew the derailleur clamp bolt and detach the derailleur from the frame.

Installation

Mount the derailleur to the frame, passing the chain between the cage plates. Position the derailleur so the cage plates are parallel to the chainrings, with about 2 mm (5/64-inch) clearance between the outer plate and the teeth of the big chainring (when the plate is over the big ring). Tighten the clamp bolt securely.

> **Note:**
>
> *If the crank-set has "Biopace" or elliptical chainrings, be sure to set this gap when the teeth under the derailleur cage are at their highest point.*

Rear derailleur

> **Note:**
>
> *Make sure the cage plates remain parallel to the chainrings when the bolt is tightened. If the derailleur moves when you tighten the bolt, compensate for this by turning the derailleur an equal amount in the opposite direction, then tightening the bolt.*

Install the spacer and screw at the rear of the cage plates, tightening the screw securely.

Thread the shift cable into the V-groove in the cable clamp. Pull the cable to eliminate slack, then tighten the clamp bolt securely. Install a cap on the end of the cable, if necessary.

Refer to Section 2b.1 and adjust the derailleur.

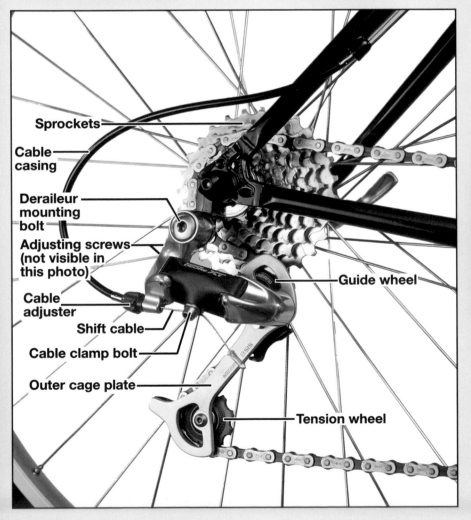

Sprockets
Cable casing
Deraileur mounting bolt
Adjusting screws (not visible in this photo)
Cable adjuster
Shift cable
Cable clamp bolt
Outer cage plate
Guide wheel
Tension wheel

2a.2 Rear derailleur
Removal

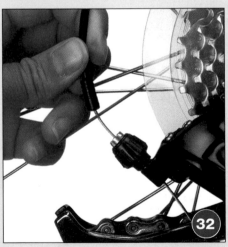

If possible, shift the chain onto the smallest rear sprocket. Pull the end cap off the shift cable, then loosen the cable clamp bolt. Pull the cable out of the adjuster.

2 Derailleurs
(continued)

Tip:

On some derailleurs the cage plates may have to be pivoted in opposite directions to make room for the chain to pass through.

Installation

33

Unscrew the bolt (and nut, on some models) and detach the tension wheel (the little "sprocket" at the bottom of the derailleur assembly) from the cage plates. This will allow removal of the derailleur without separating the chain.

34

Remove the derailleur mounting bolt. Most can be unscrewed from the outside of the bike, but some require wheel removal for access. Detach the derailleur from the bike.

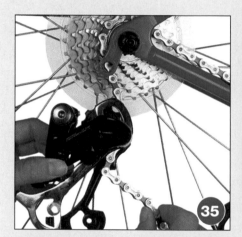

35

Position the derailleur against the frame, making sure the guide wheel engages with the chain. Install the mounting bolt and tighten it securely.

36

Align the cage plates, set the tension wheel on the chain and pull it into position. Install the bolt (and nut, if equipped) and tighten it securely.

Note:

The chain should be resting on the smallest rear sprocket.

Pass the inner cable through the hole for the adjuster and route it through the cable clamp, making sure it seats in the clamp properly (don't tighten the bolt yet). Thread the adjuster all the way into its hole and back it out two or three turns.

Pull the inner cable tight (a "fourth hand" cable puller is useful for this) and tighten the clamp bolt securely. Install a cap on the end of the cable and proceed to adjust the rear derailleur (see Section 2b.2).

2b Adjustment

Note:

The following adjustments are much easier to perform if the bike is mounted on a repair stand.

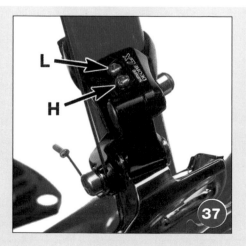

L

H

37

2b.1 Front derailleur

The first step in front derailleur adjustment is to set the low stop. This will prevent the derailleur from pulling the chain past the small chainring.

Shift the chain onto the smallest front chainring and the largest rear sprocket. Find the adjustment screws - sometimes they are marked H (for high gear) and L (for low gear), but not always. If you can't find any markings, the one on top (vertically arranged screws) or on the inside (horizontally arranged screws) should be the one for low gear adjustment.

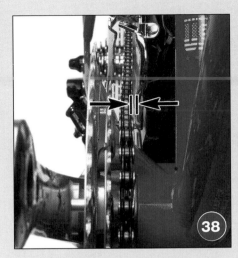

Turn the screw so you obtain a clearance of about 2 mm (5/64-inch) between the inner plate of the cage and the chain.

With the derailleur resting against its low stop, check the shift cable for slack. If there is any, loosen the cable clamp bolt, pull the cable just tight enough to eliminate any slack, then tighten the clamp bolt. If you're working on a bike with two chainrings, skip to Step 6. If you're working on a bike with a triple-ring setup, proceed to the next step.

Rotate the crank and shift to the middle chainring (triple-ring cranksets) or large chainring (double-ring cranksets). If the inner cage plate rubs against the chain, turn the cable adjuster up at the shift lever in until it stops rubbing. Turning the adjuster clockwise will allow the cage to move toward the center of the bike.

Note:

If the chain will not drop down to the smallest chainring (or makes a long clattering sound before it does), loosen the low stop and see if that was preventing it from shifting down. If that doesn't work, the shift cable is probably too tight. Try loosening the clamp bolt and slackening the cable.

After performing the steps described in the captions for photos 37 through 40, shift up to the large front chainring and the smallest rear sprocket. Adjust the other (H) stop screw to provide a 2 mm (5/64-inch) gap between the outer cage plate and the chain.

The front derailleur and indexing (on models so equipped) should now be adjusted properly. Test ride the bike to make sure that it doesn't over-shift and throw the chain off the small or big chainrings.

On index shifting systems it may be necessary to fine-tune the adjustment by turning the cable adjuster at the lever (or on the down tube if it's a road bike) if the cage plates rub on the chain in certain positions.

Guide wheels

Guide wheels (the upper "little sprocket" attached to the derailleur) on Shimano index shifting systems should have some side-to-side play in them. This helps them to align the chain on the sprockets. The guide wheel should not, however, wiggle on its axis. If it does, it's worn out.

Guide wheels on SunTour systems shouldn't have any side-to-side play in them.

2 Derailleurs
(continued)

2b.2 Rear derailleur

Derailleur stop adjustment (friction and index systems)

Shift the chain onto the second from the smallest rear sprocket and the largest front chainring. Locate the derailleur stop screws. Some are marked L (low gear - largest rear sprocket) and H (high gear - smallest rear sprocket). If you can't find any marks you'll have to experiment, because it varies from manufacturer to manufacturer.

41

Turn the H screw in a few turns and attempt to shift to the smallest sprocket - it should make some clattering sounds, but the chain shouldn't drop down. Now back the screw out, a little at a time, until the chain just drops onto the small sprocket.

42

Look at the sprockets and the guide wheel from the rear of the bike. The guide wheel should be directly under the smallest sprocket. If it isn't, turn the adjustment screw until it is.

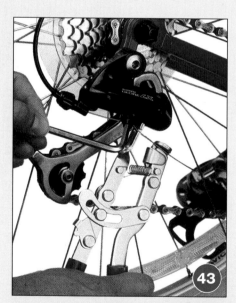

43

Tug on the rear shift cable to check for slack. Even though the derailleur is resting against its stop, there shouldn't be any slop in the cable. If there is, loosen the cable clamp bolt and pull the cable until the slack is gone. If you use a cable puller, such as a "fourth hand" tool, be careful not to pull the cable so tight that the derailleur begins to move towards the next largest sprocket. The idea is to just eliminate slack.

44

Now turn the L adjustment screw in a few turns. Downshift the front derailleur onto the smallest chainring and attempt to shift the rear derailleur to place the chain on the largest rear sprocket - it shouldn't go. Turn the L screw out, slowly, until the chain is just able to climb onto the big sprocket.

45

Again, look at the sprockets and guide wheel from the rear of the bike. The guide wheel should be directly under the largest diameter sprocket. If it isn't, turn the adjusting screw until it is. Don't turn the screw out too far, though - you don't want the chain to jump off into the spokes!

 # Shifters and derailleurs

Shift the chain to the middle chainring (triple-ring cranksets) or the inner chainring (double chainring cranksets). Turn the cranks and shift through the whole range of rear sprockets and see if the derailleur tries to throw the chain of either end of the range. If it does, adjust the stop screws accordingly. If the derailleur has a tough time shifting the chain onto the bigger sprockets, the guide wheel might not be tracking close enough to the sprockets. To cure this problem, turn the "B-tension" screw clockwise. This will move the derailleur to the rear, placing the guide wheel closer to the sprockets.

Indexing adjustment

Now it's time to adjust the indexing. If you're working on a Shimano derailleur, shift the chain onto the second smallest sprocket. If you're working on a SunTour unit, the chain should be on the smallest sprocket.

Rotate the cranks and turn the cable adjuster counterclockwise until the chain begins to rub on the next larger sprocket, then turn the adjuster clockwise just enough so the chain doesn't rub anymore. Try to downshift to the next larger sprocket - the shift should now be smooth and the chain should land on the sprocket crisply, then operate without making noise. If necessary,

play with the cable adjuster until this action is achieved.

Leave the cable adjuster at the shift lever (or down tube) alone. This adjuster should only be used to make minor trim adjustments while out riding.

Turn the cable adjuster until the chain begins to rub on the next sprocket, then back-off until the noise stops.

Keeping your derailleurs shifting smoothly

You can't expect your bike to shift smoothly if you neglect your derailleurs. Dirt, mud and lack of lubrication will slow down your derailleurs and seriously impede performance. To prevent this, you should do the following on a regular basis and whenever your bike gets dirty enough to warrant it:

Clean the derailleurs with degreaser and a brush, then rinse them off with water

Lubricate the derailleur pivot points with WD40 or equivalent

Also lubricate the guide and tension wheels of the derailleur

To prevent the shift cables from slowing down your shifts, lubricate the cables where they enter their casings (for more thorough servicing you'll have to remove the casing and clean it and the inner cable)

8

Chain and sprockets

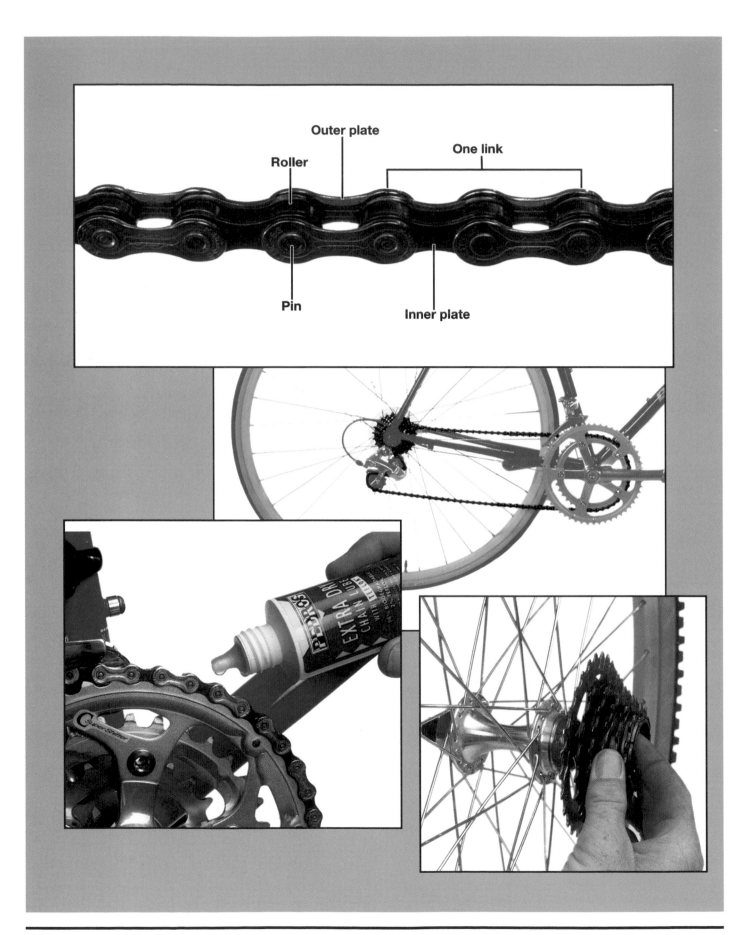

Outer plate

One link

Roller

Pin

Inner plate

8 Chain and sprockets

Contents

Introduction

This chapter covers the rear half of the power transmission to the rear wheel; the chain and rear sprockets. Included are sections on cleaning and replacing the chain, the differences of freewheels and freehubs, and sprocket replacement for both types.

1 The chain

This is the part of the bike which you'll become most familiar with, because it's the component that requires the most cleaning and maintenance. Time spent on the chain is time well spent, however, as a neglected chain will greatly reduce the performance of your bike and wear out the sprockets and chainrings faster, too. A clean chain in good condition can make all the difference between a great ride and miserable one fraught with shifting problems, noise and, perhaps, chain breakage.

1a Chain types

Basically, chains fall into two categories. The first type most of us are familiar with from our youth - the standard, 1/8-inch wide chain found on most single-speed and three-speed bikes. (This width dimension doesn't refer to the actual width of the chain, but the width of the gear teeth that it rides on.) Most of these chains have "master links" which can be removed with relative ease to allow removal of the chain from the bike. The other type of chain is the 3/32-inch chain which is used on bikes with derailleur shifting systems.

There are two different types of derailleur chain - normal (standard) or narrow (ultra). They are not interchangeable. Most standard chains (with the exception of Shimano Uniglide chains) have flat plates, with rivets that protrude from the sides of the plates approximately 1/32-inch. Narrow chains have bulging edges on their inner links, which "funnel" the

Tools you may need

A quick way to measure chain wear is with the use of this Park chain checker. Although you can measure chain wear with a ruler, this tool speeds up the process and accurately gauges the percentage of chain "stretch"

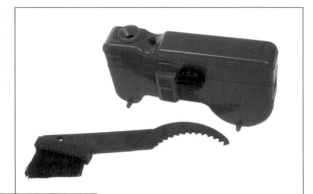

One way to keep your chain clean without removing it from the bike is with a chain cleaner such as this one from Park Tool. The brush is used for removing large chunks of debris before cleaning the chain, and for cleaning the sprockets. The toothed portion of the brush cleans the area between the sprockets

If you have to remove your freewheel or freehub, you'll most likely need a special tool that engages with the hub of the freewheel or the lockring of a freehub. Be sure to obtain the correct tool for your application

A chain "breaker" is necessary for separating derailleur chain

Anti-seize compound should be applied to the threads of the rear hub before installing a freewheel

A "chain whip" is used for immobilizing a freehub when unscrewing the lockring. Two chain whips can be used to remove the sprockets from a freewheel

A good degreaser will be required for cleaning greasy, grimy sprockets

A lightweight penetrating oil, like WD40, is good for displacing water from a wet chain and for occasional lubrication

It's best to lubricate the chain with a specific chain lubricant. Chain lubes like these are designed to keep the chain running smoothly without accumulating lots of dust and dirt

 # Chain and sprockets

Troubleshooting

Problem	Possible cause	Remedy
Bike is hard to pedal (but coasts okay)	Chain worn or in need of service	Service or replace the chain as necessary
	Bottom bracket in need of service or replacement	Service or replace bottom bracket (see Chapter 5)
Clicking, popping, squeaking or creaking noises while pedaling only	Chain dry or dirty	Clean and lubricate chain
	Chain worn out	Replace chain (and inspect sprockets and chainrings, replacing parts as necessary (see Chapter 5)
Chainrings worn	Worn-out chain	Replace chain and chainrings (see Chapter 5)
Chain is noisy (squeaky or "crunchy")	Dirty chain	Clean and lubricate chain
Chain "skips" or clicks loudly in the same spot, every revolution of the chain	The chain has a stiff link	Free-up the stiff link (see Chapter 2), lubricate the chain regularly
Chain "skips" while pedaling	Worn chain	Replace chain
	Worn sprockets	Replace sprockets and chain
Chain has too much slack (single speed bikes or bikes with hub gears)	Rear wheel not positioned properly	Adjust wheel to the rear until there is only a little slack in the chain
	Chain worn out	Replace the chain (see Chapter 8)
Freewheel makes a lot of noise while coasting	Freewheel dirty or in need of lubrication	Clean and lubricate freewheel or freehub
Freewheel doesn't spin or spins both ways	Freewheel mechanism dirty	Clean and lubricate freewheel or freehub
	Freewheel broken	Replace freewheel or freehub
Sprockets worn out	Normal wear	Replace freewheel assembly or freehub sprocket cluster (or individual sprockets). Also replace the chain.

1 The Chain
(continued)

sprocket teeth into the links of the chain, providing smoother operation and better shifting. They can also be distinguished by their chain pins, which just stick out past the chain plates (they're almost flush).

Furthermore, some of these narrow chains must be treated specially when it comes time to separate a chain link. Chains marked HG (Hyperglide), UG (Ultraglide) or NARROW require a special replacement pin for rejoining the chain links (see Section 1c.2).

When replacing your chain, bring the old one with you to the bike shop so you'll be sure to get the correct type.

1 The Chain
(continued)

1b Chain inspection and maintenance

1b.1 Inspection

Chains don't last forever. Over time, they develop small amounts of wear in each one of their little bearings. This minuscule amount of wear per bearing, multiplied by however many links there are in the chain, equals a measurable amount of chain lengthening, or "stretch." A loose, stretched-out chain will accelerate chainring and sprocket wear, leading to expensive repairs. You should monitor the wear of your chain regularly. Here's how:

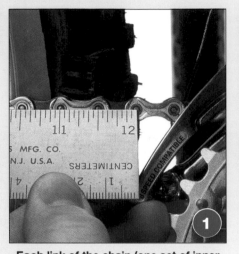

Each link of the chain (one set of inner links and one set of outer links) should measure one-inch from pin center-to-pin center. Have an assistant apply the brakes and put pressure on the pedals to tension the chain. Using a ruler, measure 12 links of the chain along the upper run, between the rear sprockets and the front chainrings. Place the left end of the ruler directly over the center of a chain pin and see where the last pin falls in relation to the 12-inch mark. If the center of the link is right on the 12-inch line, the chain is fine.

Another way to check chain wear is with a chain checker tool, such as the one made by Park Tool Company. This tool determines if a chain has stretched more than one-percent - the point at which most chain manufacturers recommend replacement of the chain. To use this tool, set the dial to the 0 position, place the tool on the chain and turn the dial until it stops. If the indicated amount of wear is still in the blue area, the chain is still good. If the dial can be turned so far that the red area shows up in the V-shaped cutout, the chain has worn past one-percent and should be replaced. This is a handy tool if you do lots of riding or have a large stable of bikes to look after.

If the chain pin falls 1/8-inch past the 12-inch mark, replace the chain.

1b.2 Maintenance
1b.2a Cleaning

Chain maintenance consists of cleaning and lubricating the chain. Cleaning can be performed by removing the chain from the bike and soaking it in degreaser or solvent, then brushing away all the grime and grease. This is a very effective method, but breaking the chain is kind of a hassle and, on some chains, requires a special replacement rivet (pin).

An alternative to this labor-intensive method is with the use of a chain cleaning tool. This will allow you to leave the chain on your bike and get it really clean.

The following procedure illustrates chain cleaning with the use of a Park ChainMate cleaning tool. Be sure to follow the manufacturer's instructions furnished with your tool. If necessary, the cleaning procedure should be repeated with fresh cleaning fluid. When finished, wipe the excess cleaner off the chain and lubricate it as described in the next section. Also, empty the dirty fluid and clean tool thoroughly.

Note:

This fluid is probably now considered "hazardous waste." Call your local waste disposal company to find out how to safely dispose of this used cleaning fluid.

Chain wear

A quick way to check for excessive chain wear without the use of any tools is to shift the chain onto the big chainring and attempt to pull the chain away from the front of the ring. If the chain can be pulled so far off the ring that an entire tooth is exposed, the chain is worn out. The chain shown here has lots of life left in it.

Place rags or newspapers on the floor under the length of the chain. Using a stiff-bristle brush, rid the chain, sprockets, derailleurs and chainrings of as much debris as possible. If it's really dirty, wash the chain with soap and water or a degreaser before using the chain cleaning tool.

Open up the cleaning tool and fill the reservoir with chain cleaning fluid. Use a citrus-based degreaser - not a petroleum-based solvent or other highly flammable liquid.

Shift the chain onto the middle chainring (triple-ring crank-sets) or the small chainring (double-ring cranksets) and the middle sprocket on the rear. Place the chain in the chain guides in the lower half of the tool and install the reservoir, turning the knob to lock it on.

Hold the tool with your left hand and slowly rotate the cranks backwards with your right hand. Depress the button on the top of the tool to let the cleaning fluid flow onto the chain. Keep doing this until the fluid reservoir is empty.

Try to apply lubricant on each roller of the chain, but at the same time use the lubricant sparingly

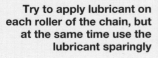

1b.2b Lubrication

The chain can be lubricated with a penetrating oil such as WD40 (or equivalent), which also displaces water after washing your bike (and can be found in almost any garage). If you use WD40, however, a special bike chain lubricant should be applied afterwards. These lubes are available in different compounds for different types of riding and riding conditions. The experts recommend a dry lube for dry conditions and a heavier wet lube for wet conditions.

1   Make sure the chain is clean and dry, as the lubricant will penetrate better.

2   Hold the spout of the bottle (or the nozzle of the can) over the front of the chainring and slowly turn the cranks backwards, taking care to apply lubricant to each roller of the chain. (If you have a one-speed bike with a coaster brake, support the bike on a repair stand or have a friend hold the back wheel off the ground for you.) Don't overdo it, though, or the chain will start dripping the lube all over the floor and the rear wheel rim (which will pretty much eliminate your rear brake).

3   Let the lubricant soak in for a couple of minutes, then wipe off the excess. The chain doesn't need to be dripping with oil to be well-lubed. On the contrary - an oily chain will hold onto all of the dirt and grime that comes into contact with it, reducing the efficiency of the chain and increasing wear, placing you right back to square one with a dirty chain.

1c Chain removal and installation

There aren't many occasions when you have to completely remove your chain from your bike. You will have to remove it if it's so dirty that a chain cleaning tool can't get it clean, or if you're stripping the frame for painting, or if you're actually replacing it with a new one.

1c.1 Standard non-derailleur chain (with master link)

Removal

Pull out the master link and remove the chain from the bike, being careful not to scratch the paint on the chainstay.

Find the master link - it's the one that looks different from all the others. Some are an elongated U-shape, others are just an oversized link plate. If the master link on your bike has a U-clip, use a pair of pliers and slide the U-clip off, then remove the plate underneath. If it has an oversized plate, flex the chain and pry it off with a screwdriver.

Tip:

If you have one of these Shimano chains and don't want to deal with the special replacement rivet, you can install a Sedisport ATB chain. It's fully compatible and requires no special replacement rivet for reassembly (and even though it says ATB, it'll work fine on road bikes, too).

Installation

Installation is the reverse of removal, with the following points:

a) If you're installing a new chain it may be necessary to shorten it. You'll need a chain breaker tool for this job (see the next Section). Remove as much chain as necessary to obtain about 1/2-inch of slack in the middle of the chain run when the rear axle is pulled half-way back into the dropout. This will give you some room for adjustment as the chain wears.

b) If your master link uses a U-clip, make sure the rounded, or U portion of the clip points in the direction of chain travel.

1c.2 Derailleur chain

Before separating your chain, determine what type it is. If you see any markings such as HG, UG or NARROW (and smooth rivet heads with no dimples), look for a black link pin. DON'T separate the chain here. These chains require slightly oversize replacement pins when rejoining them, and the black link is one of them. If you remove it, it will be a little looser when you put the chain back together. It will work for a while, but could fail under heavy pedal pressure.

If you do have one of these chains, obtain a special replacement pin from your local bike shop. And, no matter what kind of derailleur chain you have, you'll need a chain breaker tool that is compatible with your chain.

Here are some other kinds of derailleur chain that you might run across:

SunTour Pro chain - This chain has asymmetrical inner link plates (one side is flat, the other side is arched). The chain must be installed with the arched portion of the links facing the sprockets.

Regina CSX chain - Similar to the SunTour Pro, but the arched plates are only on one side of the chain. These plates should be on the inside (toward the center) of the bike.

Sedis Pro and Regina Superleggera chain - These chains have special rivets that can't be removed by a chain breaker tool. They each have about eight normal rivets so the chain can be split or shortened, if necessary. These rivets look different than the others.

Removal

Place the chain tool on the chain, with the rivet centered under the pin of the tool and the outer link plate of the chain resting on the tool.

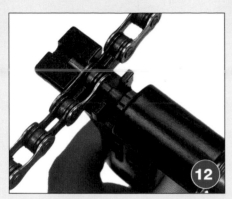

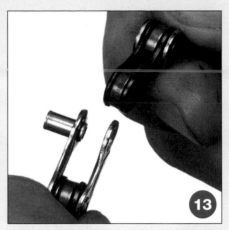

Turn the handle on the tool until the rivet just clears the inner link plate, but not so far that you push it out of the outer link plate on the opposite side of the chain (unless it's a Hyperglide, Ultraglide or a chain marked NARROW, in which case it doesn't matter). It's best to stop a little short, try to separate the chain, then push the pin out a little more if the chain won't come apart.

If you're installing a new chain, compare the length of the old chain with the new one. If necessary, remove links from the new chain to obtain the required length. Generally, the chain should be just long enough to allow you to shift it

When the rivet has been pushed through far enough, separate the chain and thread the end without the protruding rivet through the derailleurs, taking care not to scratch the paint on the chainstay.

onto the big chainring up front and the big sprocket in the rear - a gear combination that should never be used. When in this awkward gear, the rear derailleur cage should be completely extended.

Note:
Sometimes chains get lost when they break, especially when off road. If you don't have the old one, or just want to ensure the new chain is the proper length, thread it through the derailleurs and over the biggest chainring and sprocket. Pull the chain together as tight as you can, note which links touch each other, then add one full link (a set of inner plates and a set of outer plates). Break (separate) the chain here and save the extra links for a future emergency.

Installation

Route the chain into place, but rest the front portion on the bottom bracket to give yourself some working slack. Place a rag on the bottom bracket so you don't scratch the paint. Connect the ends of the chain, install the chain tool and push the rivet back into place. When assembled, the rivet should be exposed an equal amount on each side of the chain. If you pushed it through too far, reverse the chain tool and push the rivet back as necessary.

If you're joining a Hyperglide, Ultraglide or NARROW-marked chain, be sure to install the replacement rivet taper-end first. Using the chain tool, push this special rivet in until it clicks into place. The new rivet will drive out the old one if it's still in place.

Using a pair of pliers, break off the end of the rivet.

1 The chain (continued)

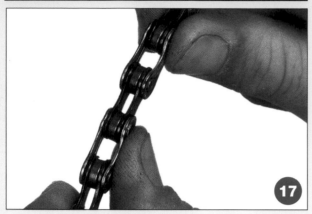

17 The link that has been joined will probably be stiff. To loosen the link, flex it back-and-forth as shown.

18 Some chain tools have an additional shelf for loosening stiff links. Set the chain on this upper shelf and turn the handle until the tool pin applies a little pressure to the rivet. Just tighten the tool a little, then remove the chain to see if it's freed-up. If not, put the chain in the tool again, this time from the opposite side, and try again.

2 Freewheels, freehubs and sprockets

2a General information

The rear sprockets are mounted to either a freewheel or freehub, inside of which lies a ratcheting mechanism. This allows you to coast, but when you pedal it then transmits all of your effort to the rear wheel through a couple of little pawls.

The freewheel assembly can either be integral with the hub (this is a freehub) or a separate unit that screws onto the hub of the wheel (this is a freewheel).

Freehubs are generally (but not always) found on more expensive bikes. They are advantageous over freewheel units in that the sprockets are easier to change and they make for a stronger wheel. The right-side axle bearing on a freehub is placed closer to the end of the axle, whereas on a freewheel rear hub the axle bearing is tucked away under the freewheel unit. This reduces the occurrence of broken axles. Freewheels have also been known to twist right off their mounting threads on the wheel hub - something that won't happen with a freehub.

To really confuse things, the freehub is sometimes referred to as a cassette freewheel.

Freewheel and freehub lubrication

Freehub

Freewheel

Every now and then it's a good idea to lubricate the freewheel or freehub with a light penetrating oil. This can be done without removing the unit from the wheel (although for a more thorough lubing the freehub or freewheel will have to be removed)

Turn the freewheel or freehub backwards and direct the spray between the moveable part of the freewheel/freehub and the internal, stationary portion.

2b.1 Freewheel removal and installation

Most riders only remove their freewheel to replace it after the sprockets wear out, the bearings wear out or it becomes damaged internally. It also must be removed to replace a drive-side spoke. However, it isn't a bad idea to remove the freewheel every once in a while to lubricate the innards.

You'll need a special freewheel remover tool to unscrew the freewheel from the hub. There are quite a few different variations, so if you don't know exactly what type of freewheel you have, take the entire wheel with you to the bike shop so you can be sure to get the proper tool.

Tip:

When replacing a freewheel assembly with a new one, it's a good idea to install a new chain, too. Worn chains will usually try to "skip" on the sprocket teeth, creating a very annoying noise and harsh operation.

How to tell the difference between a freewheel and a freehub

Freehub

Freewheel

Before you attempt to tear apart your rear hub you need to determine if you have a freewheel or a freehub. They both require a similar special tool for removal, but removing a freehub also necessitates the use of a chain whip.

Look at the area outboard of the smallest sprocket. If there is a flat, screw-on lockring that rotates with the sprockets as the sprockets are turned backwards (freewheeling), you have a freehub. There might also be an arrow on the small sprocket that indicates where the oversize spline on the freehub body is.

If you look between the smallest sprocket and the axle while turning the sprockets backwards and see a stationary central portion or "hub" with internal splines or notches in it, you have a screw-on freewheel.

Installation

Removal

Install the freewheel removal tool into the center of the freewheel, then install the axle nut or quick release skewer and nut (without the springs) to hold the tool in place. Hold the wheel securely, unscrew the tool counterclockwise until the freewheel breaks loose, then remove the axle nut or quick release. The freewheel can now be removed by hand. Check for the presence of a spacer or two under the freewheel. Make sure to install these under the new freewheel (not all units have them).

Clean the freewheel with degreaser and a stiff brush, then squirt a spray lubricant into the mechanism from the backside. Follow this up with a few drops of chain lube.

Carefully thread the freewheel onto the hub by hand. The threads on the hub are very easy to strip - if you feel any resistance at all, unscrew the unit and try again. It isn't necessary to tighten the freewheel with a wrench. The chain will pull it tight on the hub as you pedal.

Apply a film of anti-seize compound to the threads on the hub. This will make future removal easier and prevent corrosion between the hub and the freewheel.

2b.2 Freewheel sprocket replacement

The only reason to disassemble a freewheel would be to create a custom-ratio gear cluster. It makes no sense to replace worn sprockets individually, because if one sprocket is worn, it is likely all of them are. If you are putting together a custom-ratio freewheel, check on the availability of the desired sprockets first - many shops don't carry individual sprockets for freewheels. Also, check to see if you can obtain a freewheel that already contains the gear sizes you desire.

To perform this job you'll need two chain whips - something you're not going to need very often. If you de-cide you still want to tear down your freewheel, here's how:

1   Remove the wheel from the bike.
2   Wrap one chain whip around the smallest sprocket so it will pull the

freewheel counterclockwise. Wrap the other chain whip around one of the middle sprockets so it pulls in the other direction, and so the handles of both tools cross each other. **Photo 23**
3   Squeeze the handles of the tools

Note:

Some freewheel assemblies have a lockring to the outside of the smallest sprocket, similar to that of a freehub setup. A special tool is required to remove it. If your freewheel is like this, follow the procedure described in Section 2c.1.

together. If nothing happens, squeeze harder (but be careful not to get your fingers pinched between the two handles if the sprocket loosens suddenly). It usually takes quite a bit of effort to do this. Eventually, the small sprocket should unscrew.

4   Unscrew the other sprockets using the chain tool (they shouldn't be nearly as hard to take off as the first one).

5   Installation of the sprockets is the reverse of removal. Tighten each sprocket as much as possible before installing the next one.

2c.1 Freehub sprocket set removal and installation

Note: *You'll need the proper freehub remover tool and a chain whip for this procedure.*

Removal

1   Remove the rear wheel from the bike.

2   Remove the axle nut or conical nut from the end of the quick release skewer and install the correct freehub remover tool into the splines of the lockring. Reinstall the axle nut or the conical nut on the quick release skewer.

3   Wrap a chain whip around one of the middle sprockets so it pulls clockwise on the sprocket. Place a wrench on the freehub remover tool and unscrew it counterclockwise. **Photo 24**

> **Note:**
> *The lockring will make popping noises as it is unscrewed - this is normal.*

Once the lockring has been broken loose, remove the axle nut or conical nut, then continue to unscrew the lockring.

4   Take off the lockring and lift the smallest sprocket and spacer off the freehub body. Some sprocket clusters have only one separable sprocket and spacer, but others may have two or three, and the spacers may be built into the sprockets. Pay attention and lay the parts out in order as you take them off. **Photo 25**

5   Now remove the remaining sprocket cluster. **Photo 26**

Installation

6   Before installing the sprockets, it would be a good idea to remove the freehub body and thoroughly lubricate it (see Section 2c.2).

> **Tip:**
> *When replacing sprockets, make sure all of the sprockets have the same identification markings. Also, the identification marks must face outwards.*

7   Smear a little grease on the splines of the freehub body, then slide the sprocket cluster into place. Since one of the splines is wider than the rest, the sprockets will only go on one way. Install the individual sprocket(s) and spacer(s).

8   Thread the lockring onto the freehub body, then insert the remover tool into the splines. Install the quick release skewer and conical nut, then tighten the lockring securely (you don't have to use the chain whip because the freehub won't try to ratchet). When the lockring begins to get tight it'll make the same disturbing sound it made when you took it off.

9   Remove the tool and install the wheel.

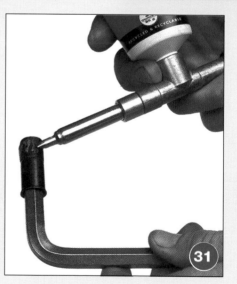

2c.2 Freehub body replacement

The freehub body will have to be replaced if the ratcheting mechanism breaks or becomes very noisy. Or, if you simply want to lubricate the freehub pawls a little more thoroughly than you can from the outside, you can take the freehub off the wheel and apply lubricant from the back.

Removal

1   Remove the wheel from the bike and take off the freehub sprockets (see Section 2c.1).

2   Remove the locknut and cone from the non-drive side of the wheel and pull the axle out of the hub (see Chapter 4). Remove the hub bearings, too. Now is a good time to inspect them, lubricating or replacing them as necessary.

3   Using a 10 mm Allen wrench, unscrew the large bolt in the center of the freehub body. **Photo 27**

4   Remove the freehub body from the wheel hub. **Photo 28**

5   If you're going to install the same freehub, clean it and apply penetrating oil to the gap between the inner and outer portions. Turn the freehub occasionally to distribute the lube all around the innards. **Photo 29**

6   Flip the freehub over and allow the excess lubricant to drain out for a few minutes. Apply a heavier lubricant, such as a wet chain lube, between the two portions of the freehub. **Photo 30**

7   Wipe off the outside of the freehub and install it onto the splined boss on the wheel hub. Lubricate the threads of the freehub bolt with grease and thread it into place, tightening it securely. **Photo 31**

8   Reinstall the sprocket cluster (Section 2c.1) and assemble the axle and bearings in the hub (see Chapter 4).

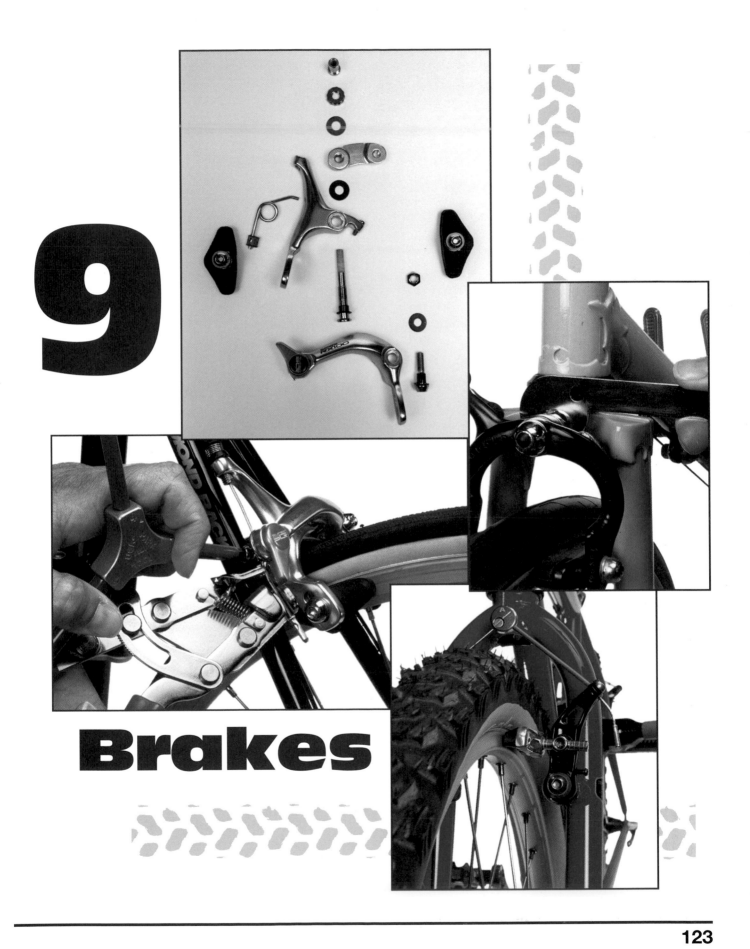

Brakes

Hood

Lever mount

Lever pivot

Lever

9 Brakes

Contents

Introduction

This chapter covers the most important part of your bike - the brake system. Brakes that don't work well are not only a danger to yourself, but can also endanger others around you.

The brakes on your bike take a minimal amount of care and maintenance, but when a problem does crop up, be sure to fix it immediately. If you inspect your brakes regularly and repair problems when they are first noticed, you most likely won't be burdened with any surprise brake problems.

Many different brake designs have been used over the years. The most prominent types on the market today are side-pull, found mostly on road bikes, and cantilever, found on almost all mountain bikes. This chapter covers those, as well as center-pull and U-brakes.

Brake types

Center-pull brake

Cantilever brake - link-wire type

Side-pull brake

U-brake

Cantilever brake - straddle-cable type

1 Inspection and maintenance

The most important points to check on the brake system are:

a) Lever reserve travel
b) Pad thickness and condition
c) Pad position on rim
d) Cable condition
e) Rim condition

The first four checks (a through d) can be found in Chapter 2. Routine lubrication of the lever pivots, brake arm pivots and cables are also included in Chapter 2.

Pad condition

Brake pads are the expendable component of the brake system. Although it takes a long time, they do wear out; a little friction material comes off every time the brakes are applied. They can also wear out with age, becoming hardened and cracked.

In some instances the lifespan of brake pads can be extended by removing them from the brake arms and sanding them flat (see Section 3 for the pad removal and installation procedure). This gets rid of any glazing and irregular wear patterns that may be present. It can also eliminate annoying squealing sounds that you can't quiet down through adjusting the pads or washing them off with rubbing alcohol. **Photos 1, 2 and 3**

Repairing brake pads

Brake pads on bicycles generally last a long time. In fact, they frequently last the life of the bike. Since replacing the pads can sometimes be a bit expensive, it may make economical sense to repair pads that are not worn excessively but are worn unevenly or glazed. Also, sanding the pads flat can sometimes eliminate brake squeal that persists after adjustment.

Glazing or minor wear irregularity can be eliminated by removing the brake pads (see Section 3) and placing them rubber-side-down on a piece of medium-grit sandpaper that's securely taped to a flat table. Move the pad in a circular pattern

If the brake pads have severe irregularities like this . . .

. . . and use a utility knife to get them as flat as possible. Final finishing should be done with sandpaper, as described earlier

Tools you may need

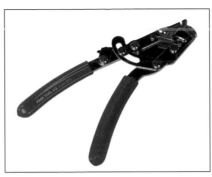

A cable puller, sometimes referred to as a "fourth hand," makes brake adjustments much easier. While a bit pricey, it can save much time and frustration

A third-hand tool will hold brake pads against the rim during cable tightening and can be substituted for a cable puller when working on side-pull brakes

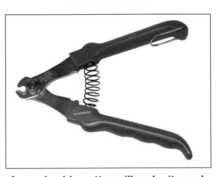

A good cable cutter will make it much easier to trim and replace frayed cables or cut new cable casing to length (cable service is covered in Chapter 6)

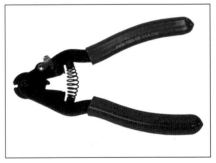

This Park cable cutter only cuts inner cables, but it's much more economical than the Shimano tool shown at left. Inner cables are replaced much more frequently than cable casings, so this tool is probably the type you should opt for

Here's a centering wrench for side-pull brakes. While not absolutely necessary, it makes centering side-pull brakes a snap

This tool is used for toeing-in the pads on side-pull brakes without having to remove the wheel

It's imperative that your brake lever mounts are tight. The problem is, most screwdrivers won't allow you to bear down on the lever mounting screw hard enough or get the screw tight without mangling its head. This special screwdriver for tightening brake lever mounts will allow you to get the mounting screw very tight without damaging the slot in the screw head

Brake tools

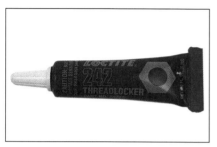

Many bikes use Allen-head screws throughout the brake system. If your bike does, this three-way Allen wrench belongs in your tool box

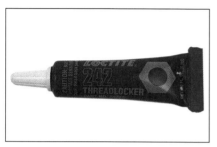

If you're installing canitlever brake arms, you should apply a drop of non-hardening thread-locking compound to each mounting screw

A light film of grease should be applied to all metal-to-metal contact surfaces. Don't overdo it, though, and be sure to not get any grease on the brake pads or the rim

Rim condition

The condition of the rims plays an important role in the braking process. When the brake levers are squeezed and the pads contact the rim, the friction between the pads and rim generates heat. This dissipation of energy is what slows the bike down. If the rims aren't in good condition, braking will suffer.

Rims that don't run true will cause pulsation and may even drag on the brake pads when the brakes aren't applied. Dented or bulged rims will cause an even more severe pulsation. If your rims exhibit any of these problems, true them up or replace them.

A clean braking surface on the rim is also very important. Sometimes a buildup of friction material on the rim (evidenced by black streaks on the side of the rim) can reduce the coefficient of friction between the pad and the rim so much that stopping distances increase greatly. Try cleaning off this buildup with a mild abrasive, such as a ScotchBrite sponge. Follow up by washing the rim with soap and water to get rid of any remaining residue. **Photo 4**

Brake test

This test may seem a bit obvious, but unless you occasionally take a moment to check adjustment, your brakes could become dangerous.

Squeeze the brake lever hard enough to apply moderate brake pressure and notice how far the lever travels. The amount of travel shown in this photo indicates the brakes are adjusted properly

If the brake lever travels this far, your brakes are in urgent need of adjustment. Generally speaking, try to adjust for at least 3/4-inch of remaining lever travel when the brakes are firmly applied

If you're replacing or adjusting brake pads, chances are you'll need a 10mm wrench (most brake pad retaining nuts are this size)

Troubleshooting

Problem	Possible cause	Remedy
Bike doesn't coast well	Brakes rubbing on rim	Adjust the brakes
	Hub bearings in need of service	Service hub bearings (see Chapter 4)
Brake pad(s) rub on rim	Brake not centered	Adjust (center) brake
	Wheel out of true	True-up wheel (see Chapter 4)
	Brake return spring(s) weak	Adjust or replace spring(s)
	Brake not returning fully due to sticky operation	Disassemble brake, clean and lubricate pivot points
	Brake not returning fully due to sticky cable	Clean and lubricate or replace cable (see Chapter 6)
Brake pads worn unevenly	Brake not adjusted properly	Replace pads and adjust brake
	Brake not centered	Adjust (center) brake
Brakes squeal	Rims and pads dirty	Clean rims and pads with rubbing alcohol (rims may have to be cleaned with a mild abrasive)
	Pads worn or hardened	Replace pads
	Wrong type of brake pad compound	Try a different type of pad
	Brake pads not toed-in	Adjust pad toe-in
Brake lever(s) hard to pull	Brake cable(s) dry	Lubricate cable(s) (see Chapter 6)
	Brake cable(s) and/or casing(s) worn	Replace cable(s) (see Chapter 6)
	Brake not properly adjusted	Adjust brakes
	Brake arms and supports corroded or dirty	Remove brake arms, clean arms and supports
	Brake lever pivot dry	Lubricate lever pivot (see Chapter 2)
Bike surges or shakes when braking	Rim dented	Repair or replace rim (see Chapter 4)
	Wheel out of true	True-up wheel (see Chapter 4)
	Brake arms loose	Tighten and, if necessary, adjust brakes
	Headset loose	Adjust headset (see Chapter 11)
Brakes ineffective	Brakes out of adjustment	Adjust brakes
	Brake pads worn or hardened	Replace pads
	Rims dirty	Clean rims with rubbing alcohol (and a mild abrasive, if necessary)
	Brake cable/casing dry, rusty or worn	Inspect cable and casing, lubricate or replace as required
Brake pads rub on tire or drop off rim when applied	Brake out of adjustment	Adjust brake immediately

2 Adjustments

The most common adjustment to the brake system is the taking up of slack in the cables. Cables stretch and brake pads wear down and, eventually, you wind up with too much play in the lever. If this slop gets bad enough the lever will hit the handlebar before the brake pads clamp the rim tight enough for them to be effective. The result will be increased stopping distances - or a very sudden stop (when you run into a large, immovable object that you couldn't avoid!).

Other adjustments, such as properly orienting the pads to the rim are normally only carried out during pad replacement. Toeing-in the pads on side-pull and center-pull brakes, which eliminates brake squeal, is also an adjustment that is normally performed during pad replacement, but may have to be repeated as the pads wear in or the brake arms bend slightly.

2a Side-pull brakes

2a.1 Cable adjustment

If you find that your brake lever travels too far before the pads engage the rim, try turning the cable adjuster at the brake counterclockwise, which will, in effect, lengthen the cable casing. This will bring the pads closer to the rim and reduce lever travel.

If this simple adjustment cures the excessive lever travel, don't proceed to the next step.

> **Note:**
>
> *The cable adjusters on some side-pull brakes have a small locknut which must be loosened before turning the adjuster. Be sure to tighten this locknut after cable adjustment.*

If you turn the adjuster out as far as it can go but there is still too much play in the brake lever, you'll have to pull the inner cable through the clamp bolt. To do this, begin by unscrewing the locknut (if equipped) all the way, then squeeze the pads and screw the adjuster all the way into the brake arm. Now unscrew the adjuster two turns.

Pull the cable through the clamp bolt enough so that the pads just clear the rim when it is turned. There's more than one way to do this:

The easiest method requires the use of a cable puller, sometimes called a "Fourth hand." Connect the tool to the cable and squeeze the handles together until the desired clearance between the pads and rim is obtained, then tighten the cable clamp bolt.

Loosen the cable clamp bolt just enough to free the cable. The pads will spread apart.

Another way is to hold the pads against the rim and pull the cable through the clamp with a pair of pliers. Tighten the clamp bolt while still holding the pads on the rim. You may have to turn the adjuster in (clockwise) to obtain some clearance between the pads and the rim. Be sure to tighten the locknut on the adjuster, if equipped.

Check the operation of the brakes carefully before riding. Fine-tune your adjustment, if necessary, by turning the cable adjuster one way or the other. Finish up by squeezing the brake lever hard to make sure the cable doesn't slip through the clamp bolt. If one of the pads is closer to the rim than the other, center the brake as described next.

2a.2 Centering the brake

When the brake lever is squeezed, the pads should contact the rim at the same time. Sometimes the brake is a little off-center when in the rest position. This will cause one pad to contact the rim before the other and can result in one pad wearing out faster than the other.

To correct this problem, the spacer that holds the return spring, or the brake mounting bolt, must be turned. In most cases the brake mounting bolt will not have to be loosened.

Some return spring spacers have slots machined into them that a thin wrench will fit. On some setups a cone wrench will work, but on others an offset wrench is necessary. Place the wrench on the flats of the spacer and turn the spacer as necessary to center the brake.

Other side-pulls can be adjusted with a tool that engages the coils of the return spring (the one shown is by Park Tool Co.). Simply place the dogs of the tool into the spring coils and turn the wrench to center the brake.

If there are no flats for a wrench or spring coils for the special tool to engage, loosen the brake caliper mounting nut on the backside of the fork and center the brake, then tighten the nut securely.

Note:

Some side-pull brakes have a small set screw on the spacer that should be loosened before centering the brake.

2a.3 Toeing-in the pads

Noisy brakes are annoying and embarrassing. If you've tried sanding the brake pads and cleaning your rims and just can't seem to get rid of that unbearable squealing, try toeing-in the pads. This is nothing more than bending the brake arms so the forward end of the pad contacts the rim first.

Attach a brake toe-in tool to the caliper arm and gently twist the arm so the forward end of the pad is about 1 mm (3/64-inch) closer to the rim than the other end. The Park tool shown in the accompanying photograph fits the arm perfectly and makes the adjustment quickly and easily. If you can't get a hold of one of these, you can use an adjustable wrench, but you'll have to remove the wheel because of the lack of clearance between the caliper arm and the rim. If you're forced to go this route you may have to remove and install the wheel a few times before you get it right.

2b Center-pull and U-brakes

2b.1 Cable adjustment

If your brake lever travels too far before the pads engage the rim, try turning the adjuster at the cable hanger counterclockwise, which will, in effect, lengthen the cable casing (if you have a U-brake, the adjuster is probably located at the brake lever mount). This will bring the pads closer to the rim and reduce lever travel. If this simple adjustment cures the excessive lever travel, don't proceed to the next step.

Note:

The cable adjuster might have a small locknut which must be loosened before turning the adjuster. Be sure to tighten this locknut after cable adjustment.

If you turn the adjuster out as far as it can go but there is still too much play in the brake lever, you'll have to pull the inner cable through the clamp bolt on the yoke that holds the straddle cable. To do this, begin by unscrewing the locknut (if equipped) all the way, then squeeze the pads against the rim and screw the adjuster all the way into the cable hanger (or, in the case of a U-brake, into the brake lever mount). Now unscrew the adjuster two turns. Have a friend hold the brake pads against the rim or, better yet, hold the pads against the rim with a C-clamp or a "Third-hand" tool.

Loosen the nut on the cable clamp bolt on the yoke while holding the clamp bolt with a wrench to prevent it from turning.

Pull the cable through the clamp bolt while pushing up on the yoke to remove all slack. Since the pads are up against the rim, it isn't necessary to use lots of force to eliminate this slack. Tighten the nut on the cable clamp bolt securely. Remove the C-clamp or Third-hand tool (or tell your friend to let go).

After following the adjustment procedure, check the brake lever travel (squeeze the lever hard to make sure the cable doesn't pull through the clamp bolt). If it is acceptable, great. If there is now not enough play in the lever, turn the adjuster screw in as necessary. If there's just a little too much play, go ahead and adjust it out by unscrewing the adjuster as discussed above. Tighten the locknut, if so equipped. Spin the wheel and make sure the pads don't drag on the rim. If they do, loosen the adjustment a little. If only one pad drags, center the brake.

2b.2 Centering the brake
Center-pull brake

To center the pads on a center-pull brake, loosen the mounting nut on the backside of the fork and turn the brake mount one way or the other so the pads are equidistant from the rim. Tighten the nut securely when you're done.

2c Cantilever brakes

2c.1 Cable adjustment

If the brake lever travels too far before the pads engage the rim, try turning the adjuster at the brake lever mount counterclockwise, which will lengthen the cable casing and take up the slack. This will bring the pads closer to the rim and reduce lever travel.

U-brake

If you have a U-brake, find the little set screw on one of the brake arms and turn it in or out to apply or release tension to that arm. In between adjustments, firmly squeeze the brake lever to center the yoke on the straddle cable - this will prevent the yoke from favoring one arm or the other (you may even have to move the yoke manually to center it).

Other types of U-brakes use spring bodies with flats machined into them that can be turned with a thin wrench to increase or decrease spring tension. If you have this type, refer to **Photo 27** for the centering procedure.

2b.3 Toeing-in the pads

Refer to Section 2a.3 for the brake pad toeing-in procedure - it's the same as for a side-pull brake.

Note:
Some U-brakes have toeing-in washers just like a cantilever brake. If yours is like this, refer to Section 3, Brake pad replacement, as this is an adjustment that is normally performed only when the pads are changed.

Note:
The cable adjuster might have a small locknut which must be loosened before turning the adjuster. Be sure to tighten this locknut after cable adjustment. 20

If this simple adjustment reduces lever travel, you're done; there's no need to continue.

If you turn the adjuster out as far as it can go but there is still too much play in the brake lever, you'll have to shorten the inner cable. To do this, begin by unscrewing the locknut (if equipped) all the way, then turn the adjuster all the way into the lever mount. Now unscrew the

If your U-brake doesn't have a set screw or flats machined into the spring bodies, detach the yoke from the straddle cable. Loosen the pivot bolts and move the pads away from the rim, then tighten the bolts. This will add more spring tension to the brake arms, holding them away from the rim. If one pad is closer to the rim than the other, loosen the pivot bolt on the arm for that pad, then move the pad a little further from the rim and tighten the bolt.

2c.1a Link-wire brake

Loosen the cable clamp bolt on the brake arm.

adjuster two turns and proceed with **Photo 21**.

After the adjustment procedure, squeeze the brake lever hard to ensure that the cable doesn't slip through the clamp bolt. If necessary, fine-tune the adjustment by turning the cable adjuster at the brake lever mount. Be sure to tighten the locknut, if so equipped.

2 Adjustments
(continued)

Pull the cable out of its fixed position slot in the cable carrier and place it in the movable position (the larger slot).

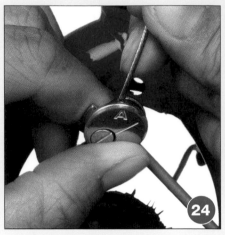

Pull the cable through the clamp until the pads are approximately 1.5 to 2 mm from the rim. The easiest way to do this is with a "Fourth-hand" cable puller, but a pair of pliers can be used instead. When the pads are properly situated, tighten the clamp bolt securely.

Move the cable back to the fixed position in the cable carrier.

Note:
Earlier model link-wire setups have a clamp bolt holding the cable carrier together. If yours has a clamp bolt, loosen the nut on the bolt so the cable can slide through.

2c.1b Straddle-cable brake

Small cable adjustments can be made by loosening the clamp bolt and pulling the cable through, but doing this may cause the yoke to contact the reflector mount. It is preferable to take up the slack at the yoke, just like adjusting the cable on a center-pull brake. Refer to Section 2b.1 for the cable adjustment procedure.

There are two basic designs of straddle-cable cantilever brakes. One type uses a straddle cable with permanent cable ends (usually they're barrel-shaped) like the one shown here. The other kind of straddle-cable setup uses a straddle cable with one permanent cable end, the other end being attached to the opposite brake arm by a clamp and bolt arrangement (very similar to a link-wire brake in this regard). To shorten the cable on this style brake follow the procedure given in Section 2b.1, since adjusting the cable in the yoke is performed in the same manner as on a center-pull brake.

Warning:
On straddle-cable brake systems and link-wire systems that have a clamp bolt through the cable carrier it is imperative that the reflector bracket be left in place. If the main brake cable should break, the reflector bracket will prevent the straddle cable (or link wire) from digging into the tire and throwing the rider over the handlebars. While this is an unlikely failure, it is one that could kill you. If your reflector bracket is missing, get one. An alternative is to install a bolt through the reflector bracket mounting hole in the fork and secure it with a nut on either side of the fork crown. Make sure the bolt is long enough to catch the straddle cable if the main cable breaks.

2c.2 Centering the brake

Cantilever brakes use one of two methods to equalize the distance between the pads and the rim. Some designs have a small screw on one of the brake arms. To increase tension on the arm, turn this screw clockwise. This will cause the pad to move away from the rim and the opposite pad to move closer to the rim. Turning the screw counterclockwise will, of course, have the opposite effect.

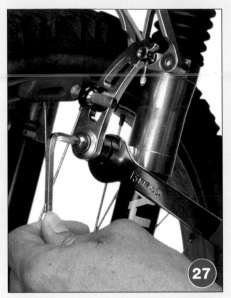

2c.3 Toeing-in the pads

Although it may become necessary to toe-in the pads occasionally as the pads wear, toeing-in the pads is normally done when replacing the brake pads. Refer to Section 3 for the brake pad replacement procedure.

If your brake doesn't have a tension screw, it'll have flats machined into the spring body, just behind the brake arm. Place a wrench on these flats, loosen the brake arm mounting screw and turn the spring body one way or the other to increase or decrease tension on the brake arm. Increasing tension will pull the pad away from the rim and move the opposite pad closer to the rim. Decreasing tension allows the pad to move in towards the rim and the other pad to move away from the rim. When you have satisfactorily centered the brake, tighten the brake arm mounting bolt securely.

3 Brake pad replacement

Brake pads normally last quite a long time, but they don't last forever. Depending on how you ride, and how often you ride, they may last anywhere from six months to three or four years. If you don't ride very often the pads can still "wear out" by becoming hardened.

When replacing your pads be sure to install original equipment pads or a high-quality aftermarket substitute. If your bike seems to take lots of effort to stop, even though everything is in proper adjustment, you should consider upgrading your pads. Replacement pads come in different compounds and lengths and can greatly enhance stopping power.

It is very important to monitor the condition of your brake pads - your survival depends a great deal on those four little inexpensive chunks of rubber or synthetic material.

3a Side-pull and center-pull brakes

Note: *This procedure also applies to U-brakes with pads that mount to slotted arms.*

Screw the cable adjuster all the way in (if yours has a locknut, loosen it first), then back it out two turns. Loosen the clamp bolt on the caliper arm (side-pull brakes) or on the straddle cable yoke (center-pull brakes) and let the brake caliper arms spread apart. (This is assuming you are replacing pads because the old ones have worn out and the cable adjuster has been unscrewed gradually over time to take up the slack. If your cable adjuster is already turned in most of the way and you are simply replacing pads to try a different compound or brand, it isn't necessary to loosen the cable clamp bolt.)

Proceed with the pad replacement sequence shown on the next page, then adjust the brake cable as described earlier in this Chapter. Fine-tune the adjustment with the cable adjuster (and be sure to tighten the locknut, if so equipped). Make sure the quick-release lever is fully closed.

3 Brake pad replacement (continued)

Remove the bolts or nuts that hold the brake pads to the caliper arms, then detach the pads from the arms. **(28)**

Install the new pad in the caliper arm and tighten the bolt or nut finger tight only, so you can adjust the position of the pad. Slide the pad up or down so it will contact the rim in the center of the braking surface and parallel with the top of the rim. It must be at least 1 mm (about 3/64-inch) away from the top of the rim or it could rub on the tire and cause a blowout. **(29)**

Note:
If the pad has directional marks on it, make sure they face in the direction of forward wheel rotation.

Once you've got the adjustment right, hold the pad in position and tighten the mounting bolt or nut securely. You might have to prevent the pad from turning by holding it steady with a pair of adjustable pliers. **(30)**

3b Cantilever and U-brakes

Some more recent cantilever brakes have pads that can be replaced without disturbing the pad holder in the cantilever arm. If your pad holders each have a small screw at the rear end of the holder, see the sidebar on page 138 for pad replacement.

Some U-brakes have pads that mount to slotted arms, as opposed to the type that have infinitely adjustable mounts (like a typical cantilever brake). If you have a U-brake with slotted arms, refer to Section 3a for the pad replacement procedure.

Turn the cable adjuster on the brake lever mount all the way in (if yours has a locknut, loosen it first), then back it out two turns.

Now refer to **Photos 31 through 36** for the pad replacement procedure. Stay in order and be sure to read the caption under each photo.

Unhook the detachable end of the link wire or straddle cable from the brake arm and let the pads spread apart. **(31)**

Loosen the clamp nut on the backside of the brake arm. **(32)**

Rotate the old pad up and pull it out of the clamp on the brake arm. **(33)**

Slide the new pad into place and adjust it to contact the rim in the center of the braking surface and so it is parallel with the top of the rim. It must be at least 1 mm (about 3/64-inch) away from the top of the rim or it could rub on the tire and cause a blowout. Also, it should be well above the inner edge of the rim or it could drop off the rim during hard braking, tearing out spokes. If the pad has directional marks on it, make sure they face in the direction of forward wheel rotation.

Also, take a look at the lines on the mounting shaft. On most brakes, two or three of these should be visible between the back of the pad holder and the clamp on the brake arm. If your pads don't have any marks like this, just be sure to insert both brake pads into the clamps the same distance.

After the new pads have been installed, connect the link wire or straddle cable to the brake arm and refer to Section 2c.1 to adjust the cable, if neces-

Now it's time to toe-in the pads. Insert an Allen wrench into the front of the pad clamp and twist the holder so the front of the pad is about 1 mm (3/64-inch) closer to the rim than the back of the pad. Tighten the clamp nut securely.

sary. When you're through, squeeze the brake lever hard a few times to make sure the pads don't slip in their clamps.

TIP

If you have a "Third-hand" tool you can use it to simplify the toeing-in procedure. Place a dime between the back end of each pad and the rim, then squeeze the pads against the rim and clamp them there with the Third hand. Make sure the pads are properly oriented on the rim and in the brake arms (see Steps 5 and 6), then tighten the clamp bolt enough to hold the pads in place (the tool will probably prevent you from inserting an Allen wrench into the brake pad clamp). Remove the tool, insert an Allen wrench into the brake pad clamp and tighten the nut on the other side of the clamp securely.

Replacing brake pads on Shimano M-System cantilevers

Shimano M-System cantilever brakes have a neat feature that allows quick and easy brake pad replacement without upsetting the orientation of the brakes. If your pad holders each have a small screw at the rear end of the holder, proceed as follows:

Loosen the set screw a few turns . . .

. . . push the pad out the rear of the holder . . .

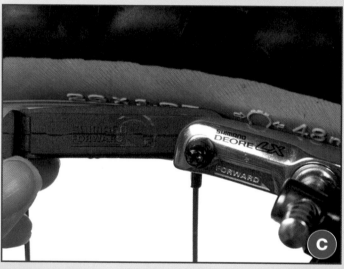

. . . slide the new pad into place, making sure the FORWARD mark is upright and faces to the front and the R or L corresponds to the side of the bike you're working on . . .

. . . then tighten the screw securely, but not too tight (it's easy to strip out the cross heads even when loosening them if they're too tight).

4 Brake assembly removal, overhaul and installation

4a Side-pull brake

Other than routine adjustment, pad replacement and checking to make sure everything is tight, brakes seldom require attention - there just isn't much that can go wrong with them. But if the brake action becomes sticky or so dirty that you just can't get it clean by normal washing methods, you can remove the brake from the bike, disassemble it for cleaning, then lubricate the pivoting parts and put it back together again. The result should be a brake that works as good as new.

Typical side-pull brake assembly

Loosen the cable clamp bolt, unscrew the cable adjuster from the caliper arm and detach the cable and casing from the brake. Unscrew the mounting nut.

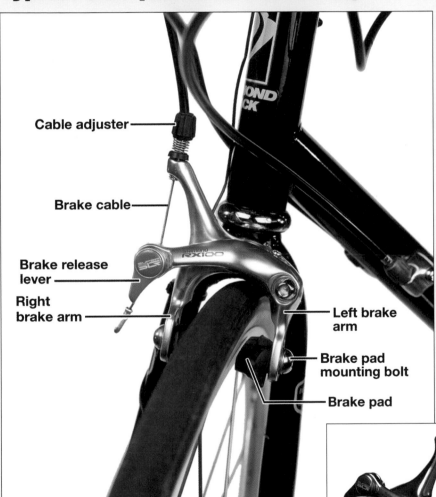

Cable adjuster

Brake cable

Brake release lever

Right brake arm

Left brake arm

Brake pad mounting bolt

Brake pad

Pull the brake away from the frame or fork.

Note:

If you're working on a Shimano dual-pivot side-pull, the outer caliper arm will have to be unbolted from the brake mount first.

Unscrew the locknut and disassemble the brake, pulling the components off the center bolt. On some brakes the components come off the front of the center bolt; others must be disassembled from the rear.

4 Brake assembly removal, overhaul and installation
(continued)

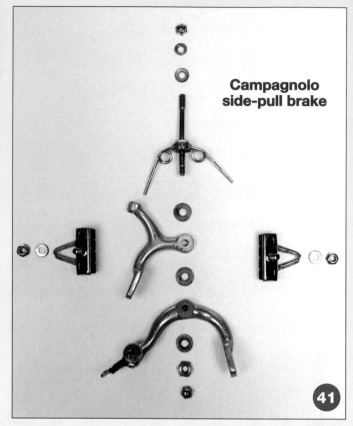

Campagnolo side-pull brake

41

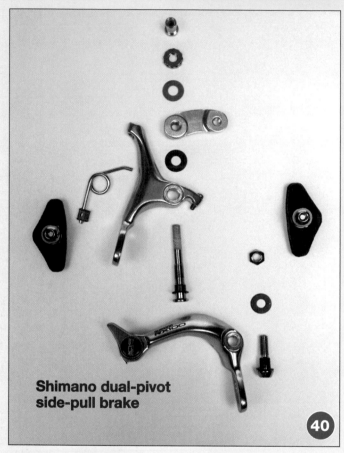

Shimano dual-pivot side-pull brake

40

Lay out the parts in order as you disassemble the brake, noting the locations of all washers, spacers and other small parts. Clean all of the components, with the exception of the brake pads, with degreaser. If the center bolt is corroded, clean it and all pivoting surfaces with fine emery cloth, then with degreaser again. The brake pads can be cleaned with fine emery cloth, followed by a wipe-down with rubbing alcohol. Assemble the brake by reversing the disassembly steps, coating all contact surfaces with a light film of grease.

42

Install the caliper on the frame or fork, center it the best you can for now and tighten the mounting nut securely. Install the brake pads (see Section 3a) then adjust the brake as described in Section 2a.

Note:

It's a good idea to put a drop of non-hardening thread-locking compound (blue Loctite or equivalent) to the threads of the center bolt.

Making sure the locknut is loose, tighten the center bolt or adjusting nut until all play between the caliper arms is eliminated, but don't tighten it so much that the arms bind - they must be able to move freely. Now hold the return spring spacer with a wrench and tighten the locknut securely (or on some designs, hold the adjuster nut stationary and tighten the locknut).

Upgrading your inadequate side-pull brakes

Many lower-end mountain bike look-alikes are equipped with cheap side-pull brakes that can be considered dangerously inadequate, especially if they aren't adjusted perfectly. The problem with these brakes is in their construction. Their scrawny caliper arms are made from softer alloys - a combination which allows the brake to flex, making it unable to squeeze the rim hard enough to affect an acceptable stopping distance. Coupled with these weak calipers on some models are weak brake levers. Again, too much flex to transmit any real power.

The only way to cure this problem

and make your bike stop well is to replace the calipers and, if necessary, the brake levers. The most cost-efficient way to do this is to install a pair of BMX side-pull brakes and levers. (In case you don't know, BMX is short for bicycle motocross.) These calipers and levers are much stouter and flex far less than the side-pulls on low-end bikes, and they are reasonably priced. Visit your local bike shop and see what they have to offer.

If you decide to go this route, you should install new cables as well. High-quality cable casings compress much less than cheap ones, and good inner cables stretch

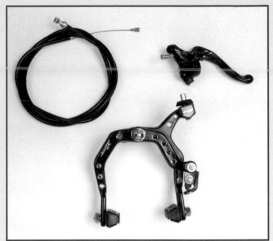

less, too. The new brakes, levers and cables will transform your bike into a real stopper. You won't believe the difference!

Center-pull brake

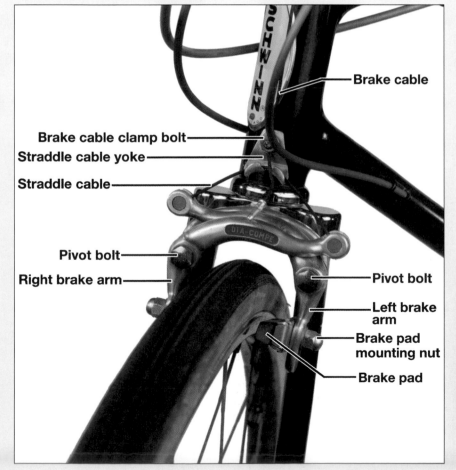

Brake cable

Brake cable clamp bolt
Straddle cable yoke
Straddle cable

Pivot bolt
Right brake arm

Pivot bolt
Left brake arm
Brake pad mounting nut
Brake pad

4b Center-pull brake

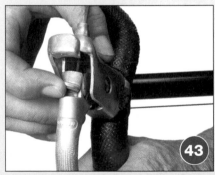

43

Engage the brake release, if equipped, to give you some slack in the cable. These are sometimes located at the brake lever.

44

Detach the straddle cable from the yoke.

Unscrew the mounting nut and lift the brake away from the frame or fork.

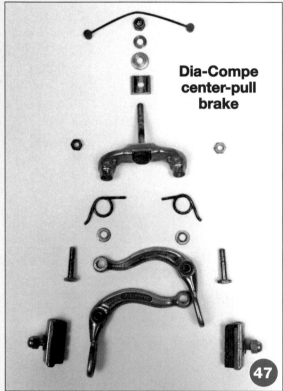

Dia-Compe center-pull brake

To dismantle the center-pull brake, remove the pivot bolts and lift the caliper arms off the mounting plate. Lay out the parts in order as you disassemble the brake, noting the locations of all washers, spacers and other small parts. Clean all of the components, with the exception of the brake pads, with degreaser. If the pivot bolts are corroded clean them and all pivoting surfaces with fine emery cloth, then with degreaser again. The brake pads can be cleaned with fine emery cloth, followed by a wipe-down with rubbing alcohol.

Cantilever brake with straddle cable

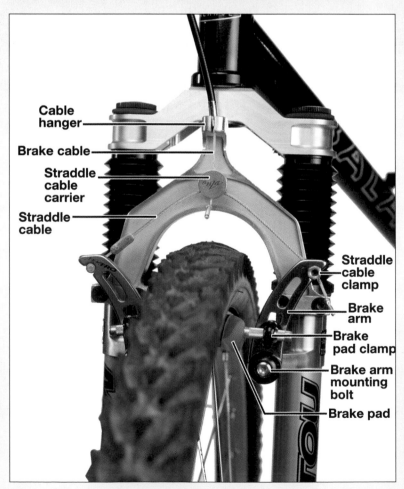

Cable hanger
Brake cable
Straddle cable carrier
Straddle cable
Straddle cable clamp
Brake arm
Brake pad clamp
Brake arm mounting bolt
Brake pad

Assemble the brake by reversing the disassembly steps, coating all contact surfaces with a light film of grease. Place a drop of non-hardening thread-locking compound (blue Loctite or equivalent) to the threads of the pivot bolts and tighten them securely.

Install the brake on the frame or fork, center it the best you can for now and tighten the mounting nut securely.

Note:

It's a good idea to put a drop of non-hardening thread-locking compound (blue Loctite or equivalent) to the threads of the mounting bolt. Install the brake pads (see Section 3a).

Connect the straddle cable to the yoke then center the brake as described in Section 2b.2. If it was necessary to loosen the cable clamp bolt, adjust the brake as described in Section 2b.1. Make sure the brake release is disengaged (in its normal position) before adjusting the cable or riding the bike.

4c Cantilever and U-brakes

1   Detach the link wire or straddle cable from the brake arm. On link-wire brakes, loosen the clamp bolt and detach the cable from the other arm.
2   Unscrew the mounting bolt and slide the cantilever assembly off its pivot post, noting which hole the tension spring end comes out of (if there's more than one).
3   If you're removing the brake to cure sticky operation, all you have to do now is clean the pivot post with fine emery cloth and degreaser, as well as the pivot hole in the brake arm. There's no real need to remove the brake pad holder from its clamp unless you just want to polish the parts so they shine. **Photo 48**

Note:

Disassemble one brake at a time so you can use the other brake for reference, if necessary.

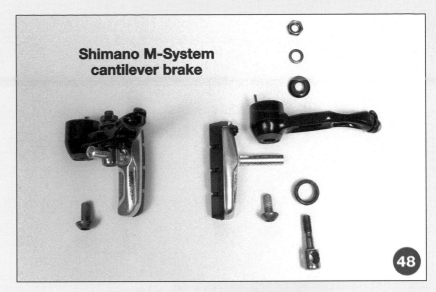

Shimano M-System cantilever brake

48

Cantilever brake with link wire

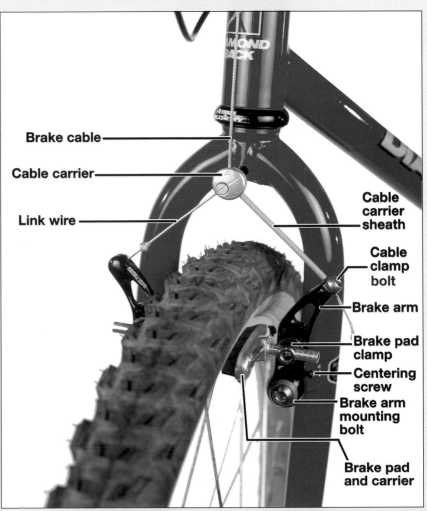

Brake cable
Cable carrier
Link wire
Cable carrier sheath
Cable clamp bolt
Brake arm
Brake pad clamp
Centering screw
Brake arm mounting bolt
Brake pad and carrier

U-brake

49

50

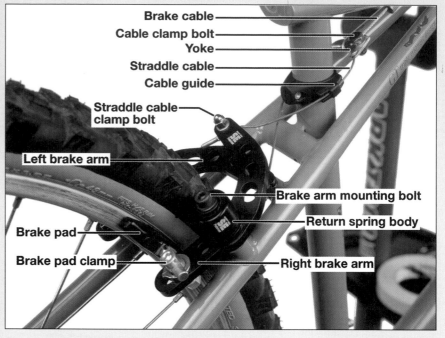

- Brake cable
- Cable clamp bolt
- Yoke
- Straddle cable
- Cable guide
- Straddle cable clamp bolt
- Left brake arm
- Brake pad
- Brake pad clamp
- Brake arm mounting bolt
- Return spring body
- Right brake arm

4　Before installing a cantilever or U-brake arm, lubricate the pivot post with a film of grease. Install the arm on the pivot post, inserting the tension spring end into the proper hole. **Photo 49**

5　Apply a drop of non-hardening thread-locking compound (blue Loctite or equivalent) to the threads of the mounting bolt, turn the bolt in by hand, then tighten it securely. **Photo 50**

6　Connect the brake cables to the cantilever arms. If you have a link-wire type brake, adjust the brake by following the procedure in Section 2c.

Aside from routine lubrication the brake levers require little attention. A brake lever is very susceptible to crash damage, though, in which case it'll have to be replaced.

Converting your link wire cantilever brakes to a straddle-cable system

Besides adding a custom touch to your bike, this modification will benefit you by simplifying the brake adjustment procedure. By eliminating the link-wire and installing a straddle cable, it is easier to center a cantilever brake.

All you have to do is detach the link wire from the cantilever arm, loosen the brake cable clamp bolt on the other arm, then pull the cable carrier and link wire off the main brake cable. Slide the new cable carrier onto the main cable and tighten the clamp screw on the carrier. Be sure the carrier doesn't interfere with the tire or, when the brake lever is pulled in completely, the cable

hanger. Now, attach the end of the straddle cable to one cantilever arm, pass the cable through the hanger and connect it to the other brake arm. Pull it through far enough to achieve the desired amount of clearance between the brake pads and the rim, then tighten the clamp bolt on the cantilever arm (check the lever travel and make sure there is adequate reserve distance between the lever and the grip).

Shown here is a cable carrier by Tektro and a "Chill Pill" by Onza. The Chill Pill is self centering, as it doesn't clamp to the straddle cable. To center the brake, increase or decrease tension on the brake arm(s).

If you're installing a cable carrier which clamps to the straddle cable, like the Tektro carrier shown here, first center the brake, then tighten the straddle cable clamp screws.

5 Brake lever removal and installation

Typical components of a road bike lever

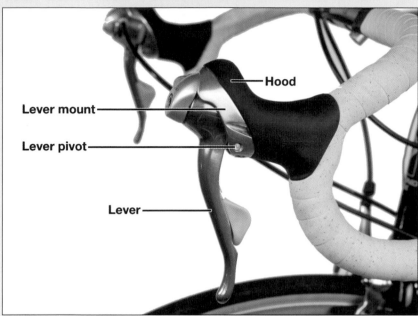

Hood

Lever mount

Lever pivot

Lever

5a Road bike levers

Note:

If you're working on a bike with STI levers (which incorporate the shifters into the brake levers) refer to Chapters 6 and 7 for the cable detachment and lever removal procedures. If you need to remove the mount also, perform the procedure described here.

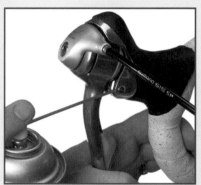

Brake lever pivots should be occasionally lubricated for smooth operation

1   Remove the handlebar tape. The best way is to simply cut the old tape off. If you're removing the levers to re-place the handlebars, leave the cables in place; otherwise, remove the brake cables from the levers.

2   Engage the brake release, if equipped. On most bikes with side-pull brakes this is mounted on the caliper arm, right below the cable ad-juster. On other bikes it's a button or lever near the top of the brake lever, sometimes on the side. If your bike doesn't have a release, turn the cable adjuster in all the way to produce slack in the cable.

3a   Pull the brake lever and insert a screwdriver into the lever mount from the front to loosen the clamp screw. If there isn't enough slack in the cable you'll have to loosen the cable clamp bolt at the brake (see Section 2b.1, if necessary). **Photo 51**

3b   If you're removing an STI lever mount, the clamp bolt is concealed by the lever hood. Peel back the lever hood to expose the clamp bolt on the outer side of the mount. **Photo 52**

4   Once the screw has been loos-ened adequately, slide the mount off the handlebar.

5   Installation is the reverse of re-

moval, but be sure to position the lever where it is easy to operate from the tops of the bar and also with your hands on the drops (see Chapter 1, if necessary). **Photo 53**

6   Install new handlebar tape (see Chapter 11).

7   Disengage the brake release or, if you turned the cable adjuster or loos-ened the cable clamp bolt, adjust the brake (see Section 2b.1, if necessary).

51

52

53

5 Brake lever removal and installation
(continued)

5b Mountain bike and hybrid levers

Typical components of a mountain bike lever

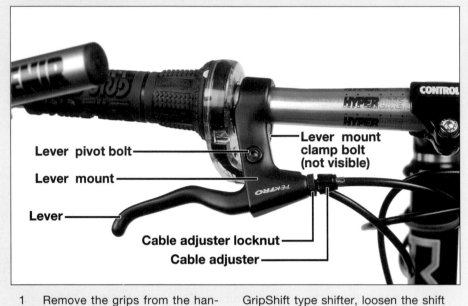

Lever pivot bolt

Lever mount

Lever

Lever mount clamp bolt (not visible)

Cable adjuster locknut

Cable adjuster

Note:

Some brake levers can be removed from their mounts and replaced separately; the lever removal procedure is usually self-evident. Others cannot be replaced individually and require removal of the entire mount from the handlebar.

Occasionally squirt some WD40 (or equivalent) into the brake lever and cable pivots

1   Remove the grips from the handlebar (see Chapter 11). If you plan on installing new grips, simply cut off the old ones. If you're removing the levers to replace the handlebars, leave the cables in place; otherwise, remove the brake cables from the levers (see Chapter 6).

2   If your bike is equipped with a

Note:

On Shimano levers with integral shifter housings this will mean removing the shift cables, too.

GripShift type shifter, loosen the shift housing clamp screw and slide the shifter off the handlebar (see Chapter 7).

3a   The location of the lever mount clamp screw or bolt varies. Some are inside the mount, requiring the link-wire or straddle cable to be detached to produce some slack in the cable. The lever can then be pulled and a screwdriver inserted to loosen the screw. **Photo 54**

3b   The clamp screw on other brake lever mounts is usually behind or underneath the lever. **Photo 55**

4   Once the clamp screw has been loosened, slide the lever and mount off the bar.

5   Installation is the reverse of removal, but be sure to adjust the lever position so it's in line with your forearm when you're seated on the bike. **Photo 56** Tighten the clamp screw securely.

(54)

(55)

(56)

10

Seat and seat post

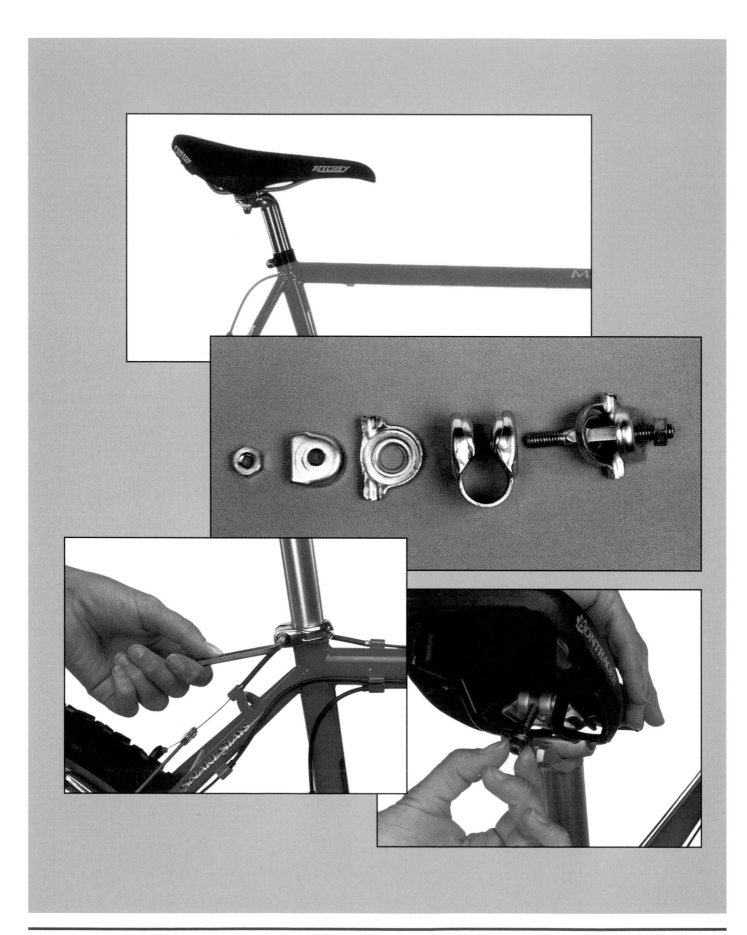

10 Seat and seat post

Contents

Introduction

Most of your riding time is spent "in the saddle." For some this creates a problem - a sore rear end. The seat is, without a doubt, the most cussed-at part of the bicycle. This derision is quite unfair most of the time, as a simple adjustment or two would probably correct the discomfort (see Chapter 1 to find out how to properly set up your seat).

If adjusting the seat doesn't help, try a new one. Seats come in a huge variety of designs and materials, including extra-wide models that look almost like tractor seats and styles specifically for the female anatomy. As a last resort you can wrap your seat with a gel-filled cover to add an extra bit of padding.

1 Maintenance

1   The seat and post require very little maintenance. Leather seats should be regularly treated with saddle soap or some other leather preservative. Also, leather seats can "sag" over time and must be tensioned if this happens. To do this, tighten the nut underneath the nose of the seat to stretch the leather. **Photo 1**

2   The seat post doesn't require any maintenance whatsoever - just make sure it's adequately greased. Otherwise, water seeping in between the post and the frame can cause corrosion that will fuse the post to the frame and make it extremely difficult to remove. **Photo 2**

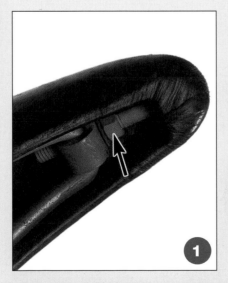

Getting your seat post to move smoothly

Most mountain bikes are equipped with a quick release on the seat post clamp. This is good, but you'll find that on some bikes, mainly lower-end mountain bikes, the seat height is still difficult to adjust with the quick release open. This is because the top of the seat tube on the frame was never de-burred, and it's usually worse on seat tubes that have a slightly fishmouthed opening. This can cause gouging of the seat post if it's bad enough.

To correct this problem, remove the seat post (and the clamp, if it's detachable) and, using a half-round file, chamfer the inner circumference of the seat tube.

Clean up the seat post with fine emery cloth. If there are any burrs on the post, remove them with a file.

Wipe away all metal filings, lubricate the seat post with grease and slide it into place. Before closing the quick release lever, give it a shot of penetrating oil (WD40 or equivalent) to keep it working smoothly.

Troubleshooting

Problem	Possible cause	Remedy
Seat post seized in seat tube	Seat post corroded	Apply penetrating oil around the post, wait awhile, then try to remove it. If you still can't remove it, take the bike to a bike shop.
Seat won't maintain position	Seat clamp loose or worn	Tighten or replace seat clamp (see Chapter 10)
	Seat post loose	Tighten seat post clamp
	Wrong size seat post	Be sure your post is the correct diameter for your seat tube

2 Adjustments

1   There are two basic designs of seat post and retention methods for attaching the seat to the post. The most common and inexpensive type is with the multi-piece seat clamp. This kind of clamp fits over the top of the seat post, which is narrower, and grips the seat rails between four pressed-metal components. A fifth piece of the clamp fits between the rails and holds everything else to the post. A threaded stud runs through all five components, and a nut on each side tightens the clamp. This kind of post and clamp is

relatively heavy and offers only coarse seat angle adjustments. **Photo 3**

2   The other type is the micro-adjustable type, of which

there are two versions. One really isn't micro-adjustable, but it offers a finer adjustment than the clamp type. It uses only one bolt to secure the clamp plate and is much simpler and lighter than the clamp type. The true micro-adjustable post uses two bolts to secure the clamp plate and is infinitely adjustable. **Photo 4**

2a Seat height

5

Loosen the seat post clamp bolt or quick release. If your bike has a clamp with a hex head on both sides of the clamp, chances are that only one side will turn (the other side will have a tab to hold it stationary).

2b Seat tilt and fore/aft positioning

Setting the proper seat tilt is a major factor affecting your riding enjoyment. If the nose of the seat is too low, your weight is shifted forward and puts too much pressure on your shoulders, arms and wrists. If the nose of the seat is too high, you'll probably experience lots of discomfort and end up with a painful bruise in a sensitive location(!)

This is an adjustment that may take a little experimentation to find the best angle for your body. Start by adjusting the seat so it is level. You can use a bubble level to determine this or, if the top tube of your bike's frame is basically level, adjust the seat parallel with the top tube. Ride your bike a few times with the seat in this position before you decide to change the angle - each time you make an adjustment it'll take a little time to get used to it. Of course, if the seat is just downright painful at this setting, ignore this advice.

The fore and aft position of the seat can be adjusted also. Most seat and clamp combinations allow for at least two inches of front-to-rear movement. To determine where the seat should be positioned, refer to Chapter 1, Section 2c.

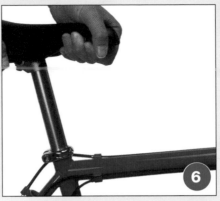

6

Adjust the seat to the desired height. You may have to twist it back and forth to get it to move. If the post is stuck, spray it with penetrating oil (WD40 or equivalent), wait a few minutes for the oil to soak in, then try again.

Caution:
If you just can't get the seat post to move, take the bike to your local bike shop and let them get it unstuck for you.

7

If the seat post is dry, be sure to lube it up with grease. Also smear some grease inside of the seat tube of the frame. Now take a look at the post to make sure you haven't raised it up past the minimum insertion, or maximum height mark. If you have, you'll need a longer seat post. When you're finished with the adjustment, tighten the clamp bolt or quick release.

Warning:
Never ride with the seat post raised past the minimum insertion mark.

2b.1 Clamp-type seat post

8

Loosen the nut on the seat clamp. Normally you'll only have to loosen the nut on one side of the clamp, as both nuts are threaded onto the same stud.

9

If necessary, the seat can be moved forward or backward on its rails. When you've adjusted the seat where you want it, make sure the nose of the seat is pointing straight ahead then tighten the clamp nut securely.

2 Adjustments (continued)

2b.2 Micro-adjustable seat post

If your post only has one bolt like the one shown here, loosen it enough to allow the seat to be moved on the rocker portion of the post. The seat can also be moved from front to rear with this bolt loosened.

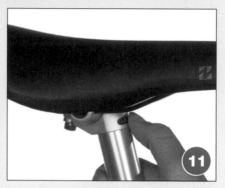

Some posts (the truly micro-adjustable kind) have two clamp bolts to secure the rocker. The one shown here has a little thumbwheel to turn the forward bolt, which you will turn to adjust the angle of the seat once the rearmost bolt has been loosened.

Other posts have two clamp bolts, but their heads are a little harder to get at. To tilt the nose of the seat forward on this type, loosen the front bolt and tighten the rear one. Do just the opposite if you need to raise the nose of the seat.

3 Seat removal and installation

The only time it becomes necessary to remove the seat is if you're replacing the seat or the seat post.

3a Clamp-type seat post

Loosen one of the seat clamp nuts, then pull the seat and clamp off the post. Loosen up the nut a little more if necessary, then detach the clamp from the seat rails.

3b Micro-adjustable seat post

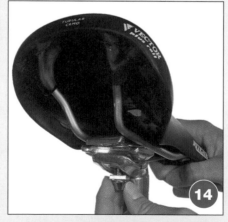

If your seat post only has one seat clamp bolt, loosen it a few turns and turn the clamp plate 90-degrees so it fits between the seat rails. Lift the seat off.

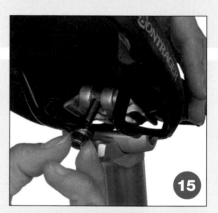

If you have a micro-adjustable seat post with two bolts or a thumbwheel that turns the forward bolt, loosen the rear bolt and swing it outwards, then lift the clamp plate up off the seat rails and remove the seat.

If you have a seat post with both bolt heads hidden under the seat, loosen them up far enough to allow the seat rails to be detached from the two halves of the clamp, then remove the seat.

Installation is the reverse of removal, with the following points:

It's a good idea to lubricate the threads of the clamp bolts with grease, especially if they thread into an aluminum clamp.

Be sure to adjust the angle and the fore/aft position of the seat, then tighten the bolt(s) securely.

11

Steering

11 Steering

Contents

Introduction

This Chapter deals with the components that have the greatest effect over the control of your bike - the handlebar and grips, the stem, the headset and the fork.

1 Handlebars

1a Grip replacement

Grips are a common replacement item and it's also necessary to remove them when removing the brake levers, shifters or handlebar.

1   Remove the bar ends if your bike has them. They're usually secured by a single clamp bolt.

2   If you're removing the grips to install new ones, cut the old ones off with a knife or razor blade. If you intend to re-use them, insert a long, thin screwdriver under the grip and squirt some soapy water between the grip and the handlebar. Twist the grip back and forth to loosen it up, then pull it off the end of the bar. **Photo 1**

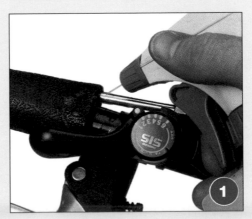

Note:
If the grips won't slide off you can spray a little penetrating oil (WD40 or equivalent) between the grip and the bar, but you'll have to remove all traces of oil from the bar and install new grips (it isn't a good idea to use the old ones if you had to resort to this method, unless you are absolutely sure you can clean out all of the penetrating oil from the inside of the grips. A loose grip can cause a crash).

Troubleshooting

Problem	Possible cause	Remedy
Bike feels shaky or wobbly	Loose headset bearings	Adjust the headset
	Loose hub bearings	Adjust the hub bearings (see Chapter 4)
Clicking, popping, squeaking or creaking noises while pedaling only	Loose handlebar binder bolt (pedaling under heavy load, pulling on bars)	Tighten binder bolt
	Stem bolt loose (pedaling under heavy load, pulling on bars)	Tighten stem bolt
	Stem rusty or dry in steerer tube (pedaling under heavy load, pulling on bars)	Remove stem, clean and lubricate
Bike pulls to one side (especially when you let go of the handlebars)	Forks bent	Replace forks
	Frame bent	Have the frame straightened or replace frame
Bike surges or shakes when braking	Headset loose	Adjust headset
Steering feels loose in some positions and tight in others	Bent fork steerer tube	Replace the steerer tube (if possible, and this is a job for a bike shop) or the entire fork (in this case a bike shop will probably have to cut the steerer tube to the proper length)
Steering fells "notchy"	Headset bearing races damaged	Replace headset
Too much effort required to turn handlebars	Headset bearings too tight	Adjust headset
	Headset bearings in need of service	Disassemble, clean and inspect the headset bearings and races. Lubricate or replace as necessary
Front end rattles over bumps	Loose headset	Adjust headset
Headset keeps loosening up	Threads on steerer tube damaged	Replace the steerer tube (if possible, and this is a job for a bike shop) or the entire fork (in this case a bike shop will probably have to cut the steerer tube to the proper length)
	Headset locknut not tightened securely	Tighten securely with proper headset wrenches (not pliers!)
Stem seized in steerer tube	Stem corroded	Apply penetrating oil around the stem, wait awhile, then try to remove it. If you still can't remove it, take the bike to a bike shop. Be sure to lubricate the stem with grease when reinstalling

1 Handlebars
(continued)

3 Clean the handlebar thoroughly, using degreaser if you had to apply penetrating oil.

4 To install the grip onto the bar you'll probably have to apply something slippery to get it to slide on. Saliva works well, and some people use hair spray - it acts as a lubricant when wet, but dries like a glue. Whatever you use, don't ride the bike until the grips have dried and are firmly in place on the bar. Slide the grip into place.

5 If you're installing bar ends, use a hammer and tap the end of the grip against the handlebar to cut a circle out of the end of the grip, then continue to slide the grip inwards far enough to accommodate the bar end. Remove the circle of rubber from the

end of the handlebar. If your bike didn't have bar ends before, you'll probably have to loosen the brake and shift lever mounts and move them in towards the stem to make room for the bar ends. Be sure to tighten them securely after you've moved them. **Photo 2**

Warning:

If you aren't installing bar ends, be sure the end of the handlebar is covered by the grip, or install a plug. Never ride with the handlebar end exposed or unplugged - you could be impaled if you crash and land on the end of the handlebar.

6 If you're installing a bar end, mount it on the handlebar at the desired angle, then tighten the clamp bolt just tight enough to prevent the bar end from slipping on the bar. If you tighten the clamp bolt too tight, the handlebar could be crushed.

Tools you may need

If you're going to adjust or overhaul your headset, you should use a pair of wrenches made specifically for this purpose. Be sure to get the proper size for your headset

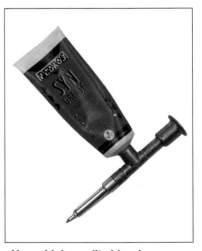

A tubing cutter can be used for trimming a threadless steerer tube to length (however, this may be a job you should leave to a bike shop mechanic)

Although special tools are available, a hammer and large drift can be used for removing headset races from the head tube

You'll need a good degreaser for removing the old grease from headset bearings and races

Use a high-quality bicycle grease when lubing headset bearings. The grease injector shown here allows you to apply grease with pinpoint accuracy

1 Handlebars
(continued)

1b Tape replacement

Handlebar tape on a road bike bar eventually becomes worn and dirty over time, and replacing it is a great way to rejuvenate your bike's looks. It'll also have to be removed and replaced if you're removing the brake levers or handlebar (you most likely won't get good results trying to wrap a handlebar with used tape).

Note:

It's OK to start the tape from the end of the handlebar and finish at the top of the bar.

Take out the plugs from the ends of the handlebar. If your bike has bar-end shifters, refer to Chapter 7 for the shifter removal procedure.

If your brake lever mounts are covered with rubber hoods, peel the hoods back to expose the tape. Unwrap the tape or remove the padding from the bar. If your brake cables run underneath the tape, make sure they are secured to the bar with short pieces of electrical tape.

Make sure the brake lever mounts are adjusted properly and are tight (see Chapter 9, if necessary). Clean off the old glue from the handlebar and cut a piece of tape from each roll to cover the inside and outside surfaces of the mounts, where the mounts clamp to the bar. Stick these small pieces of tape into place on the mounts.

Starting out from the stem a couple of inches, begin winding the tape around the bar. Wrap the tape around the bar one time, then pull it at an angle, overlapping about one-third to one-half the width of the tape as you wrap the bar.

When you come to the brake lever mount, wrap the tape around the underside of the mount, then back over the top, like a figure-eight. Make sure the short pieces of tape are covering the area where the mount and the bar meet.

Proceed to wrap the bar all the way to the end, then give it one more wrap to overlap the end of the bar. If the tape isn't long enough you have overlapped it too tightly - unwind it and try again. Trim off any excess tape, but leave about 1/4-inch hanging over the end of the bar.

Tuck this overhanging tape into the end of the bar and install the end plug (or shifter). If you started at the end of the bar, wrap the tape over the last wrap around the bar, then trim the excess off at an angle so it is parallel to the edge of the stem.

Most replacement tape comes with two short lengths of finishing tape. Wrap these pieces around the edge of the tape where you ended to keep it from coming loose or peeling back.

Note:

If you're raising the handlebar on a mountain bike or hybrid and the brake cable is supported by a cable hanger or roller attached to the stem, loosen the brake cable at the brake arm (link-wire brake) or at the yoke (straddle cable brake).

1c Adjustment

The handlebar can be adjusted up or down (on bikes with standard stems) by raising or lowering the stem, or it can be rotated in the stem to change its angle. Setting up your handlebar properly has a great deal to do with your riding comfort and your control of the bicycle.

To adjust the angle of your handlebar, simply loosen the clamp bolt at the front of the stem and set your handlebar where you want it (if necessary, refer to Chapter 1 for the proper positioning of the handlebar). Tighten the clamp bolt securely. If necessary, readjust the angle of the brake levers and shifters so they're easy to operate (see Chapters 9 and 7).

To adjust the height of your handlebar, loosen the stem bolt and raise or lower the stem to set the handlebar at the desired position. When the height of the bar is set where you want it, check to be sure the stem is pointing straight ahead, then tighten the stem bolt securely. If you had to loosen the brake cable, adjust the brakes (see Chapter 9).

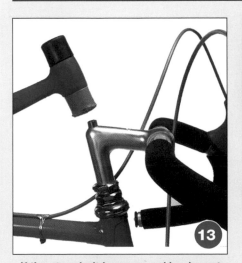

If the stem bolt loosens and backs out but the stem still won't move up or down, tap on the stem bolt with a soft-face hammer (or a regular hammer and a block of wood) to jar loose the locking wedge at the bottom of the stem.

Warning:

Don't raise the stem up past the maximum height marking! Photo 14

1 Handlebars
(continued)

1d Removal and installation

Remove the grips or the handlebar tape (see Section 1a or 1b).

Remove the brake levers and shift levers from the handlebar (see Chapters 9 and 7), then refer to **Photos 15 and 16**.

To install the bar, reverse the removal procedure. Make sure the handlebar is perfectly centered in the stem, then tighten the clamp bolt securely.

15

Loosen the clamp bolt and slide the handlebar out of the stem. If the stem is still tight around the handlebar, remove the clamp bolt and screw it back into the threaded part of the clamp. Insert a penny between the screw and the other side of the clamp, then tighten the screw to spread the clamp apart. You should be able to easily slide the bar through the stem now. This method is neater than prying with a screwdriver, but it won't work on all stems.

16

Some stems have handlebar clamps that are retained with two bolts and are completely separable. Just unscrew the bolts, detach the clamp shell and remove the bar from the stem.

2 Stem removal and installation

2a Standard type

1   Remove the handlebar (see Section 1d).

Note: If you're removing the stem for access to the headset, it isn't necessary to remove the handlebar from the stem.

2   Loosen the stem bolt and withdraw the stem from the steerer tube. If the stem sticks, tap on the bolt to free the wedge at the bottom of the stem as shown previously.

17

3   Before installing the stem, remove all rust and corrosion. Lubricate the threads of the stem bolt, the sides and top of the wedge and the shaft of the stem with grease, then insert it into the steerer tube. Adjust it to the desired

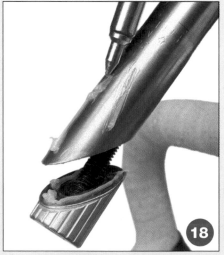

18

position and tighten the bolt snugly. **Photos 17 and 18**

4   Install the handlebar and the shift and brake levers.

2b Aheadset-type

1   Remove the handlebar (see Section 1d).

Note: *If you're removing the stem for access to the headset, it isn't necessary to remove the handlebar from the stem.*

2   Remove the bolt in the center of the stem cap. **Photo 19**

3   If the bike is secured on a work stand with the front wheel off the ground, support the wheel (or the fork if the wheel has been removed) and loosen the stem clamp bolt(s). Some stems have two, some have one. Some, like the one shown in the accompanying photo, are hidden under a cover which must be pried out. The fork can slide right out of the headset now, so be sure to support it. **Photo 20**

4   Lift the stem off the steerer tube. If you removed the stem for access to the headset bearings, refer to Section 3b.

5   Before installing the stem, lubricate the steerer tube with a light film of grease. Install the stem on the steerer

tube and line it up with the wheel.

6   Install the stem cap and bolt, tightening the bolt just enough to take the play out of the headset bearings. To do this, apply the front brake and attempt to push the bike back and forth, feeling for play in the headset. When all the play is taken up, stop tightening the bolt.

7   Tighten the stem clamp bolt(s) securely. If the stem isn't pointing straight ahead, loosen the clamp bolt(s) and tap it one way or the other so it's straight.

Caution:

The stem cap bolt does not secure the stem - it simply preloads the headset bearings. Don't overtighten it!

8   Install the handlebar if you removed it.

---

3 Headset

The headset supports the fork in the frame and allows it to turn back and forth. It is comprised of bearing races pressed into the head tube, a bearing race pressed onto the fork steerer tube, an adjustable upper race and two sets of ball bearings. On standard headsets the upper race is threaded onto the steerer tube and secured by a locknut. On Aheadset-style headsets the steerer tube is not threaded. The bolt at the top of the stem does not secure the stem to the steerer tube like a standard headset; it just takes the play out of the bearing. A clamp bolt (or bolts) bind the stem to the steerer tube.

3a Adjustment

Headsets have a habit of working loose over time, at which point they have to be adjusted. A loose headset will cause a very noticeable "clunk" felt through the handlebar when riding

over bumps or stopping quickly. This play must be taken out as soon as possible or the bearings will pound little depressions in the races, which will cause the steering to feel notchy when the headset is adjusted, as the ball bearings pass over the small detents they have made.

3a.1 Standard type

To perform this procedure you'll need a pair of headset wrenches. These wrenches are fairly inexpensive and are the only way to adjust the headset without damaging the flats on the locknut. Be sure to get the correct sizes - most bikes with 1-inch headsets (this dimension refers to the outside diameter of the fork steerer tube) require 30 or 32 mm wrenches. Bikes with 1-1/8 inch headsets usually require 36 mm wrenches. Bikes with oversize headsets (1-1/4 inch) have 40 mm flats. Take note - the flats of the bearing cup are not always the same as the flats of the locknut. It's best to measure the nuts with a vernier caliper before purchasing the wrenches.

Headset bearing check

To check for a loose headset, straddle the bike, pull the front brake lever in and rock the bike back and forth. If you feel any slop, the headset must be adjusted.

A headset that is too tight will cause stiff steering and strange handling characteristics.

3 Headset (continued)

Place the headset wrenches on the upper bearing cup and the locknut in such a way that they can be squeezed together, then loosen the locknut.

Adjust the bearing by turning the upper bearing cup. Apply the brake and rock the bike back and forth to feel for play in the headset. When you have removed all play, stop tightening the bearing cup - you don't want to preload the bearing.

Hold the bearing cup stationary and tighten the locknut down hard. Recheck your adjustment. There should be no slop in the headset bearings, but the handlebar should turn smoothly from side to side.

3a.2 Aheadset type

Loosen the stem clamp bolt(s) enough so you can turn the stem independently of the fork.

Note:

If the stem is stuck to the steerer tube and won't move, you'll have to remove the stem (see Section 2b), clean and lube the steerer tube and inside of the stem, then put the stem back on.

Tighten the Allen bolt in the stem cap enough to take up all freeplay in the headset bearings. Check this by applying the front brake and rocking the bike back and forth. Stop tightening the bolt when you don't feel any more "clunking" from the headset. With all the play removed, tighten the stem clamp bolt(s). Recheck your adjustment. There should be no slop in the headset bearings, but the handlebar should turn smoothly from side to side.

3b Overhaul

About every six months you should disassemble the headset to clean, inspect and re-lube the bearings. By doing this you'll slow down wear and lengthen the life of your headset.

3b.1 Standard type
Disassembly

1   Support the bike on a workstand, if you have one. If not, hang the front of the bike on a rope looped over the rafters. Remove the front wheel, then remove the stem (see Section 2a). It isn't necessary to remove the handlebar from the stem - you can tape or zip-tie the bar and stem to the frame. Loosen up any cables necessary to create slack to allow removal of the bar and stem.

Unscrew the headset locknut and remove the lock washer, then unscrew the upper bearing cup from the steerer tube. Support the fork with your other hand, because it will slide right out of the head tube when you remove the upper bearing cup.

Remove the fork and lift the lower headset bearings off the lower bearing race on top of the fork crown, noting how they are oriented. If the bearings are stuck in the bottom cup on the frame, retrieve them.

Lift the upper bearings off the upper race, again noting how they're installed.

Cleaning and inspection

Thoroughly clean the bearings, races and cups with degreaser. Check the ball bearings for pitting and roughness, replacing them if necessary.

> **Tip:**
>
> *Take the old bearings with you to the bike shop so you'll be sure to get the correct size replacement bearings.*

Check the bearing cups and races, too. A thin line or shiny track around the area where the bearings ride is acceptable, but flaking, uneven wear or depressed areas will warrant replacement of the headset.

Grasp the bearing cup and inner race on the head tube and try to move them. If they are loose, either they are worn out or the openings in the head tube of the frame are distorted. Take the bike to a bike shop and let them decide on the proper course of action to take.

Place the upper bearings in the threaded cup and turn the cup down the steerer tube until there is no freeplay.

Reassembly

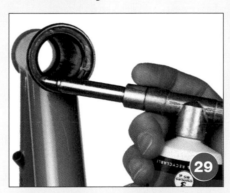

Apply a bead of grease to the lower bearing cup on the head tube. Install the lower bearings into the cup, then cover them with more grease. Make sure the cage doesn't interfere with the bearing cup and that it won't interfere with the inner race on the steerer tube. If there was a seal present, be sure to install it now.

Prepare the upper bearing, inner race and threaded cup for installation by thoroughly lubricating them with grease. Install the fork.

> **Note:**
>
> *Make sure you install the bearings in the cup with the correct side up - the cage must not interfere with the inner race or the cup. Also, if the upper cup has a seal, be sure to install it.*

Install the lock washer and locknut, but don't tighten the locknut yet. Install the front wheel.

Install the stem (see Section 2a), then proceed to adjust the headset bearings as described in Section 3a. If it was necessary to loosen up any cables, adjust them by referring to the appropriate chapter.

Installing loose ball bearings

Many bicycle mechanics prefer to scrap the bearing cages and install loose ball bearings instead. By doing this, more bearings can be placed into the bearing cups. This means the loads imposed on the headset bearings are spread out over more surface area, and the result will be a headset that is less prone to "indexing" - the condition that causes notchy steering.

To determine the amount of balls that you can put in, fill the greased bearing cups with ball bearings of the correct size. When the cup is filled with ball bearings touching each other all the way around the cup, remove two of the balls.

3b.2 Aheadset type

Disassembly

1   Support the bike on a workstand, if you have one. If not, hang the front of the bike on a rope looped over the rafters. Remove the wheel.

2   Support the fork with one hand, then remove the stem by referring to Section 2b. Leave the handlebar attached - you can tape or zip-tie the bar and stem to the frame. Loosen up any cables necessary to create slack to allow removal of the bar and stem.

3   Remove any spacers that may be present, the brake cable hanger (if equipped), the dust seal and the conical expansion washer from the steerer tube. If your headset is equipped with a snap-ring above the conical washer it'll have to be removed first. **Photo 32**

4   Lift the upper bearing cup off, then remove the fork from the frame. **Photo 33**

Cleaning, inspection and reassembly

5   Cleaning and inspection is carried out in the same manner as for a standard-type headset - refer to the previous section.

6   Be sure to thoroughly lubricate the bearings, cups and inner races, then assemble the headset by reversing the disassembly procedure. Install the stem and bar (see Section 2b), then adjust the headset by following the procedure given in Section 3a.2. If it was necessary to loosen up any cables, adjust them by referring to the appropriate chapter.

Tip:
This snap-ring really isn't necessary - all it does is prevent the fork from sliding out of the headset when the stem is removed. It can, however, prevent the stem cap bolt from taking up all of the slack in the bearings when adjusting the headset. Many experts omit this snap-ring during reassembly.

(34)

(35)

(36)

(37)

3c Replacement

A headset needs to be replaced when the steering becomes indexed or "notchy," a condition usually caused by riding over rough terrain with a loose headset. Shops use a special press to install the new bearing cup and race in the head tube, but if you're careful and work slowly you can drive them in with a hammer and a block of wood.

If you're swapping your standard headset for an Aheadset-type headset, or if you're just replacing your headset with a different brand (it may be a little shorter or a little taller), you should take your bike to the local bike shop and let them handle the conversion. They'll have all the tools required for the job and, if you're going the Aheadset route, will be able to safely remove your threaded steerer tube from your fork and install a threadless tube (and trim it to the proper length), or set you up with a new fork if your steerer tube isn't replaceable.

If you're going to attempt headset replacement yourself, take the fork and old headset with you to the bike shop when you go to buy the new headset so you can be sure to get the correct parts.

1　Disassemble the headset (see

Section 3b).

2　Using a large diameter drift made from a soft metal such as brass or aluminum, drive the race and/or cups out of the head tube. **Photo 34**

3　Set the new upper race into position on the head tube. The other side of the head tube should be resting on a flat piece of wood, perpendicular to it. Place a short scrap of two-by-four over the race and gently drive it into the head tube. Be sure it goes in straight and all the way. **Photo 35**

4　Flip the frame over and position the lower bearing cup in the underside of the head tube. Drive it into place with the hammer and wood block, again making sure it goes in straight and all the way. **Photo 36**

Note:

If you have a long tube or pipe that fits over the steerer tube and contacts the bearing race somewhere other than the bearing surface, you can use it instead of the punch - it'll drive the race on more evenly.

5　Remove the bearing race from the fork crown by tapping on it with a hammer and punch, alternating sides so it doesn't get cocked. **Photo 37**

6　Install the new race onto the steerer tube and slide it down to the crown. Tap it home with the hammer and large punch, again alternating sides so it doesn't get cocked or distorted.

7　That's all there is to it. Refer to Section 3b for the headset reassembly procedure, if necessary.

4 Fork maintenance, removal and installation

Fork removal is a part of headset overhaul. Refer to Section 3b for the proper procedure.

Standard forks require no maintenance aside from periodic inspections for cracks, bending or other damage. If any damage is found, replace it immediately.

If it becomes necessary to install a new fork (or if you're upgrading to a suspension fork), take the old one with you to the bike shop. The mechanic at the shop will match up a new fork with your old one, and will probably have to trim the steerer tube to length and clean up the threads afterwards. This isn't something you should try at home - the shop most likely has all the tools required to do the job properly. They'll also take the bearing race off the old steerer tube and install it on the new fork (provided the race is in good condition).

Suspension forks

Unlike rigid forks, suspension forks do require periodic maintenance. At the very least they'll need a shot of lubricant (WD40 or equivalent) applied to each fork leg from time to time. If your fork is equipped with dust boots, you'll have to peel the bottom of the boot away from the fork slider and lift it up. After the lube has been applied, stretch the boot around the slider, making sure it seats properly.

There are many different suspension forks on the market and most of them fall into two categories, according to their damping mechanisms: elastomer or air/oil. Elastomer-damped forks don't require any service other than slider lubrication, unless the elastomers (small urethane or synthetic rubber cylinders) lose their spring or become damaged. Forks that use air and oil have to be rebuilt occasionally, as the seals wear out over time and the damping capability of the fork will be reduced.

Service information for suspension forks has not been included in this manual since there are so many different types available. When you purchase a suspension fork you'll also receive an owner's manual with a complete set of adjustment and overhaul procedures. These instructions not only show you how to rebuild your forks, they'll provide you with the proper

setup specifications to tune your fork for your weight and riding style. If you don't have the proper owner's manual, contact the fork manufacturer to obtain one, or check with your local bike shop for assistance.

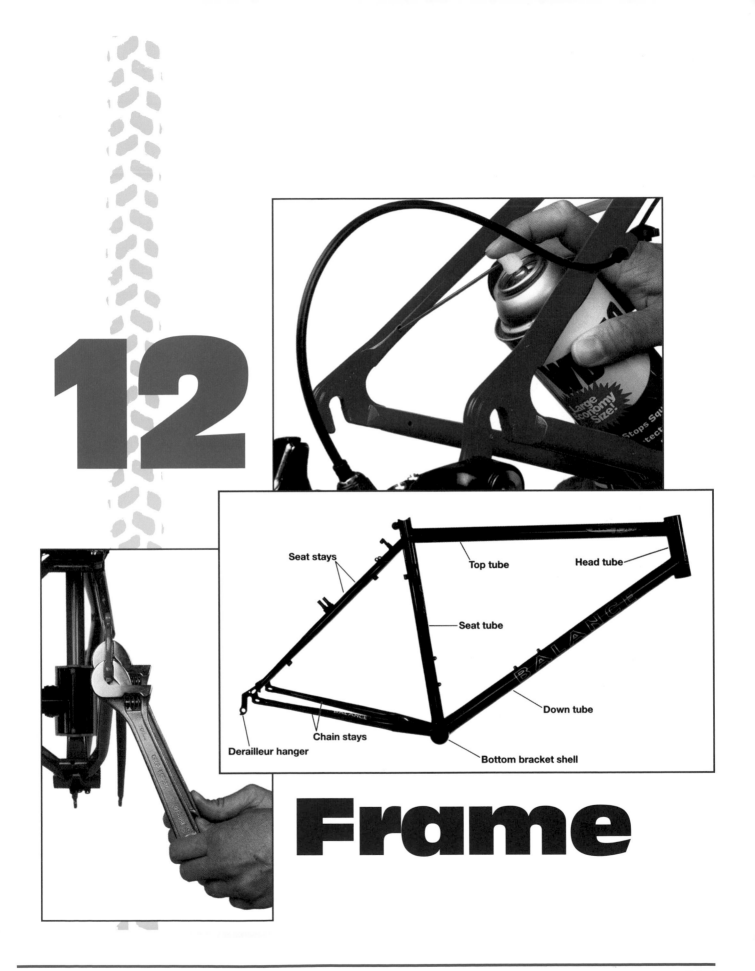

12

Seat stays

Top tube

Head tube

Seat tube

BALANCE

Down tube

Derailleur hanger

Chain stays

Bottom bracket shell

Frame

12 Frame

Inspection

The frame is the skeleton of your bike. There's not much that can go wrong with a frame, unless you crash and bend it or ride so hard that the loads imposed on it are just too much, causing it to break. In some climates rust can be a problem.

Photo 1

Before every ride (and certainly after a hard ride) you should inspect the frame for cracks, especially in the area where the top tube and down tube meet the head tube. Also check around the chain stays and bottom bracket shell. These areas are subjected to the greatest loads; if the frame is going to fail, chances are it'll happen

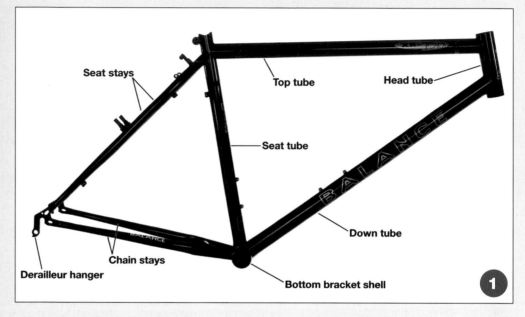

Seat stays · Top tube · Head tube · Seat tube · Down tube · Chain stays · Derailleur hanger · Bottom bracket shell · **1**

in one of these places. Sometimes cracks show up as a very fine break or scratch in the paint.

Dents in the frame tubes usually aren't a problem unless they exceed about 1/2-inch in depth. Deeper than that and the frame tube is probably weakened and possibly bent, too.

Frame cracks

Get in the habit of routinely checking your frame for cracks, especially in the areas where the top tube and down tube meet the head tube. Frames are most susceptible to damage in these areas, and a failure here could mean disaster!

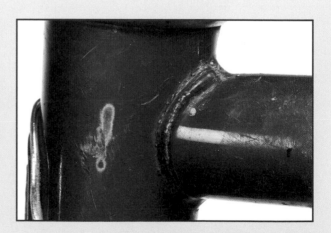

Maintenance

Frame maintenance is very simple. Just keep it clean so it's easy to check for cracks, and periodically squirt some kind of rust inhibitor (such as WD40 or equivalent) into the small holes in the chain stays and seat stays. **Photo 2**

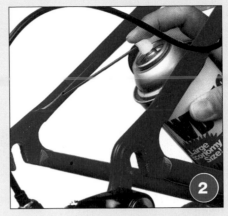

Tip:

Don't plug these holes - they allow any moisture that's present in the tubes to evaporate. If you plug them in an attempt to keep water out you'll actually prevent condensation from evaporating.

Another way to keep rust from invading your frame is to touch up nicks and scratches with clear nail polish or automotive touch-up paint. Before applying, clean the surface with lacquer thinner then apply a couple of coats of the nail polish or paint to the affected area. **Photo 3**

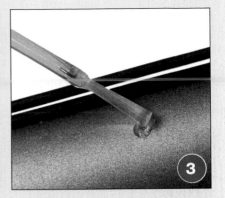

Tip:

Many car dealership parts departments carry touch-up paint - you can check to see if they have a close match for the paint on your bike.

Repair

Frame repair should be left to a frame specialist or a mechanic at a good bike shop that has the tools and expertise to perform the repair correctly. Even if you have a cracked steel frame and are a competent welder, it's easy to blow holes in the thin, hard tubing that is used for frame construction. By attempting repair yourself you may well ruin a frame that could be fixed inexpensively by someone knowledgeable in this field.

Keep in mind that some types of frame damage simply can't be repaired. Major kinks in the frame tubing caused by running into something head-on, for example, will require replacement of the frame. To straighten out a sharp bend would work-harden the metal and cause it to become dangerously brittle.

Remove the rear wheel and the derailleur (see Chapters 4 and 7). Position one adjustable wrench over the dropout for the axle and the other wrench (or locking pliers) onto the hanger, at a 90-degree angle to the bend. Slowly bend the hanger back into place.

Note:

If you have shifting problems even after straightening the hanger, have it properly straightened by a bike shop mechanic or a frame specialist.

Straightening-out a rear derailleur hanger

The part of the frame that the rear derailleur bolts to is very vulnerable. If you lay the bike down (i.e. crash) on its right side there's a strong possibility that the derailleur hanger will get bent. Most aluminum frames have replaceable hangers, but on steel frames it's part of the rear wheel dropout.

A bent derailleur hanger will cause shifting problems, especially on indexed shifter systems. With the use of two adjustable wrenches (or an adjustable wrench and a pair of locking pliers) you can usually straighten a bent hanger good enough to restore shifting to an acceptable level, or at least good enough to get you home.

You can use a straightedge placed on the dropout to determine if the hanger is straight, or you can swivel the wrench on the hanger down alongside of the wrench on the dropout - when the two wrenches are parallel the hanger is straight.

Trail rules

Just when you're ready to have some fun out in the dirt you get slapped with more rules. But by following these rules you'll ensure everyone's enjoyment, not just your own. It's important that all mountain bikers follow these rules, as it will help to keep the trails open and keep us in good standing with other trail users. Really, these rules are no more than common sense and common courtesy.

- **Don't ride where you're not supposed to.** Stay off private property and obey all signs marking areas that are off limits to cyclists. Also, as much fun as it might be, don't ride in State or Federal wilderness areas.

- **Leave the land as you found it.** When you've left the area, the only thing you should leave behind are your tire tracks. Use good judgement - if the ground is muddy, don't ride; you'll make deep ruts which will eventually harden and leave a rough (and possibly hazardous) surface. Stay on the trails, too. There are plenty of trails to ride on without blazing new ones. Be sure to carry out all litter that you create (and if you want to do a good deed, pick up

any litter that you come across). Be sure to leave gates as you found them, or if the gate has a sign on it, comply with whatever the sign says (some people don't close gates after passing through them. Others may close gates when the landowner actually wants to keep them open).

- **Give other trail users the right-of-way.** There has been an ongoing dispute amongst trail users as to who belongs there and who doesn't. If the mountain biking community shows respect and courtesy to hikers and equestrians, we stand a far better chance of being able to enjoy our sport in the years to come, and to keep the trails open for our children. When you ride up behind hikers or horses, give them plenty of room, announce your presence politely and pass slowly so as not to startle them. When you approach an equestrian from the opposite direction, stop your bike when the horse nears you so it won't get frightened and bolt.

- **Don't scare the animals!** Whether it be horses, cattle or wild animals like deer, rabbits or coyotes, leave them

alone. Remember, you're visiting their home, so treat them with respect. Besides, startling animals can be dangerous. Loud noises or your sudden appearance can trigger an animal's defensive instinct, which means bad news for you.

- **Don't ride "over your head."** Sometimes the trails start to resemble ski runs, with a few irresponsible riders going so fast that they're barely able to maintain control of their bikes. They'd never be able to stop to avoid another trail user if they had to. Most collisions on the trail are caused by such individuals and the results are occasionally tragic. You should only ride fast in areas where you can clearly see a good distance ahead - never on trails with blind corners or rises high enough that prevent you from seeing what's on the other side.

- **Be prepared.** Carry everything you think you may need to repair your bike should it break down. Know how to make basic repairs and keep your bike in good mechanical condition to minimize the chances of becoming stranded. Always let someone know where you're going, and ride with a friend whenever possible.

How to survive on the road

Far more dangerous than aggressive mountain biking is riding on the road. You might be a top-notch cyclist, but you're at the mercy of the motorists sharing the road with you. Under the best of conditions there are only a few feet of space between cyclist and car, and this distance can decrease to a few inches on narrow roads and in heavy traffic. Your survival depends on your ability to react to the circumstances that unfold before you, and as previously stated, the ability of motorists to control their vehicles. By following a few simple rules you can lessen the possibility of being injured or killed in a collision with a motor vehicle, and at the same time improve motorist-cyclist relations.

- **Always ride with the flow of traffic, on the right-hand side of the road.** Stay as far to the right as possible without actually riding in the gutter or the dirt. If there's a bike lane, *stay in it!* A cyclist riding outside of a clearly marked bike lane is sure to infuriate drivers. If you're riding with a friend, ride single file so it's easy for cars to pass.

- **Don't break the law.** If you come to an intersection with a stop sign, STOP. Rolling through a stop sign or not waiting until it is your turn to proceed are two more ways to make drivers mad. Plus, doing so could put you in the hospital (or worse).

- **Don't be unpredictable.** Ride in a straight line without swerving, and let your intentions be known through the use of hand signals.

- **Concentrate on what's happening in front of you.** Be prepared to react to obstacles, cars pulling out from driveways or turning into them, pedestrians crossing the street and so on. Don't ride over drainage grates - most narrow tires will fit right between them, which will cause a crash. Also, think about your ride - many cyclists have run into the rear of parked vehicles while immersed in deep thought or daydreaming. This is not only embarrassing, it can hurt!

- **Be mindful of what's happening behind you.** This is where your ears come into play. It's good to be able to sense when cars approach so you'll know not to swerve to the left for any reason. Small mirrors that mount on your handlebar or helmet are available to enable you to see to the rear without turning your head.

- **Don't ride too close to parked cars.** Give yourself enough room to be able to avoid opening doors and to keep your handlebar from catching on side-view mirrors.

- **Be noticeable.** Wear bright clothing so you can be seen easily. If you ride at night, use a bright headlight and tail light *and* clothing with reflective strips on it.

- **Don't be a belligerent biker.** Don't get into a shouting match over right-of-way issues (or anything else, for that matter). Don't give people "the finger" either. These actions aren't polite, won't clear up any disagreement, make all cyclists look bad, and unfortunately in this day and age it could be enough to get yourself shot!

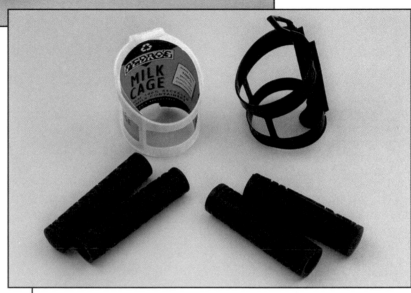

Accessories

Accessories

Introduction

The cost of cycling rarely ends with the purchase of your bicycle. Even if you have the discipline to limit yourself to one bike, there are many accessories out there that'll help you lighten your pocketbook. Some of these items are really necessities, especially if you plan on venturing out into the hills or embarking on a long road trip.

The following products represent a selection of goods that you're likely to find in most any good bike shop. You'll want to outfit your bike with some of these things right from the start. Some of the others can wait until you're ready for more aggressive riding. One thing is for certain, though - if you're serious about cycling it's almost impossible to resist the urge to upgrade, modify or customize your bike!

Wear protection! If you don't have a bike helmet, go buy one *now*. Make sure you strap it on before every ride. Modern cycling helmets are not uncomfortable and they don't look goofy like the ones of a few years ago, so don't use those points as excuses for not wearing one (as if those are valid excuses!). Helmets save lives. If a potentially fatal or debilitating head injury can be limited to a mere headache, isn't the "inconvenience" of wearing a helmet worth it?

If you have a child who rides, insist that he or she wears a helmet when riding. Many states now have laws requiring children under a certain age to wear a helmet, which is good. If all kids are required to wear helmets, there's no reason for any of them to feel embarrassed by being different. When they grow up they can decide for themselves if they want to wear one or not, but a youngster shouldn't be left to make such an important decision. As a parent, set a good example by wearing one yourself.

The helmets shown here are the Avenir Corsair (left) and the Avenir VSR Comp (right). Other good brands include Bell, Specialized, Giro and Troy Lee.

It's also a good idea to wear gloves while riding. If you've ever gone down on the palms of your hands you already know this. Gloves also reduce fatigue and eliminate slippery grips caused by sweat.The Avenir Amara gloves shown here have a padded, leather-like palm and a Lycra and terrycloth back.

Here's another item that is more necessity than accessory - a water bottle (or two). Of course, you'll also need a bottle cage to carry the bottle. Dehydration not only makes you feel lousy, it can be dangerous.

If you're buying a water bottle cage for a mountain bike, make sure it's durable enough to handle all the bumps and jolts that you will encounter. Some bottle cages are really meant only for road bike use, but models like this Mountain Race Cage from Avenir are made from larger diameter aluminum rod.

Unless you like walking and carrying your bike better than you like riding, always carry a good pump. Some people prefer a full-size frame pump, but compact units like Avenir's Air Max Twistlock are lighter. This one will inflate your tires just about as fast as a full-size pump, because it pumps air when you pull the handle out as well as when you push it in. Don't forget to carry a spare tube, tire levers and a patch kit, too.

Travel light - Under-seat packs are a great way to carry all of your essentials: spare tube, tools, money, etc. Cannondale offers this Creme de Comp pack made from recycled plastic. Unique features of this bag include a pocket on the underside to store a compact pump and a mounting plate on the back for an LED tail light.

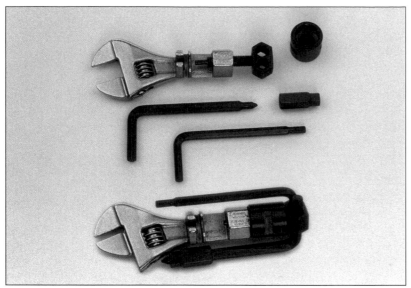

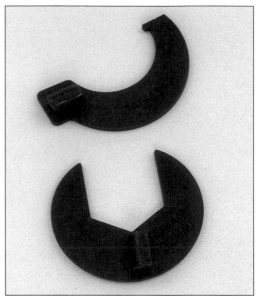

There will come a time when you break something out on the trail, or something comes loose or out of adjustment, and you'll have to fix it before continuing. To do this you'll need tools, but you really don't want to lug the toolbox along with you or listen to a bunch or wrenches clanging around in your pack. The Cool Tool solves this problem. It is aptly named, as it combines Allen wrenches, an adjustable wrench, crank bolt sockets, Phillips screwdriver, a chain breaker (compatible with Hyperglide chains), a chainring nut driver (on some models) and a spoke wrench. It doesn't end there, though - you can use it as a tire lever, derailleur hanger straightener, chainring straightener, pedal wrench, an emergency crank bolt, and even a bottle opener! Cool, indeed.

Also available for the Cool Tool are headset and bottom bracket lockring adapters, which increase its versatility.

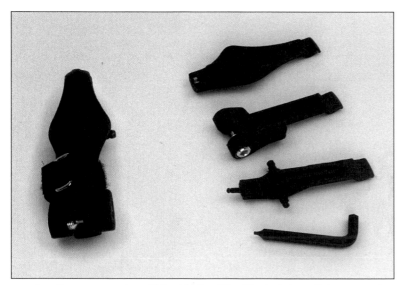

Another compact multi-tool is the Giro Pocketshop. It incorporates four Allen wrenches, two spoke wrenches (14 and 15 gauge), a chain breaker (Hyperglide compatible), a small standard screwdriver for derailleur adjustments and three tire levers - eleven tools altogether (counting each tire lever separately). It's also very light, tipping the scale at slightly less than 65 grams!

Flat tires are annoying. They aren't very challenging to fix (some riders enjoy difficult trailside repairs), but they stop you in your tracks and waste valuable riding time. To prevent flats, install a sealant such as Slime in your tubes. This sticky substance seals up punctures as they occur, which allows you to keep on pedaling. If you use Presta valves, tubes are available with Slime already installed in them. Once applied, the Slime is good for the life of the tires!

Another way to store loose items is with Avenir's Shoulder Pack. You can stuff 60 cubic inches of gear inside, and it doubles as a pad when you have to shoulder your bike and hike over obstacles.

Panniers are the cyclist's equivalent of the saddlebag. They're great for road trips, carrying goods from the market or commuting. Cannondale's Briefcase Pannier goes a step further - it's geared for the commuting businessman or student. Unique features of this pannier are: loops to store your seat and post (so nobody steals them off your bike), a water bottle pouch, briefcase-like handles, external and internal pockets, a padded lining designed to protect your laptop computer, a rain cover and a concealable, quick-release mounting system which enables you to attach it to most any rack.

Racks are a handy way to transport bulky items. You don't necessarily want a rack on your bike all the time, though. Standard racks are attached to the bike in four places and take a while to mount or remove. The Utility-X rack from Headland Bicycle Accessories is an extremely durable carrier that attaches to the bike in *one* spot - it clamps to the seat post with two Allen bolts. All you have to do is remove the seat post, slide the Utility-X rack onto the post, install the post and tighten the clamp bolts. It'll carry up to 40 pounds and has a storage compartment inside of its main beam that's large enough to hold a mini pump or small tools. It can also be used on full-suspension bikes, whereas other racks can't.

The Terrapac 250 from Cannondale is great for commuters and mountain bikers not wishing to attach a rack to their bike. It has pouches for two water bottles, a mount for an LED tail light, reflective strips, a place to store your helmet when you get off the bike, fully adjustable shoulder and abdomen straps, a zippered panel which hides pockets, penholders and a tethered keyring holder. And that's just the external stuff. Inside there's plenty of room for clothes, books or whatever you feel the need to carry. The part that rests against your back is heavily padded to prevent the contents of the pack from digging into your back.

It's always fun to see how far you've ridden, how fast you're going or have gone, and what time it is so you aren't late for dinner! You can monitor all of these critical bits of information, and more, with most cycle computers. Shown here is the AV-1 by Avenir, which gives you current speed, average speed, maximum speed, trip distance, accumulated distance (odometer), elapsed time and current time. Cycle computers are great training aids.

Leaving your bike parked anywhere is risky, but you can greatly reduce the chances of your bike getting stolen by securing it to something immovable with a good lock. U-locks have been very popular with cyclists for the past few years. As a result, thieves have become quite familiar with them, too. Avenir's Failsafe lock is a beefier version of the old U-lock, with an improved locking mechanism. Unlike standard U-locks, the bar can be inserted in either direction, and locked with the push of a button.

Grips play an important role in the control of your bike, as your hands are constantly in contact with them. Many different compounds, shapes and textures are available for you to experiment with. Most riders seem to settle on one type of grip when they've found one they like, but it's fun to try different kinds from time to time. The grips shown here are Ule's from Onza. They have finger grooves and are slightly padded to absorb shock and reduce fatigue. They also come with end plugs which will reduce your chances of being impaled should you land on the end of the handlebar in a crash.

The other parts of your body that hopefully remain in contact with your bike are your feet. One way to ensure this is with some kind of foot retention system. Some riders go for the traditional toe clip and strap setup, but these can be dangerous if they're cinched down too tight or if you just can't get your foot out due to the situation that you may be in. That's why many cyclists, including mountain bikers, are switching over to clipless-type pedals. This kind of pedal secures your foot, but a twist of the ankle is all that's necessary to get out of them. The pedals shown here are Onza's H.O. Pedals. They are compatible with SPD shoes and come with different durometer elastomers which enable you to adjust the release tension. They have replaceable sealed bearings and are available with either titanium or chromoly spindles.

If you don't want to be locked to your bike as securely as you would be with clipless pedals or toe-clips and straps, your other alternative is to use Power Grips. These heavy-duty straps bolt to your pedals and cross over them diagonally. They are easy to get into - all you do is insert your foot at a slight angle. When you straighten your foot, the strap gets tighter and you reap the benefits of being secured to your pedals. They're easy to get out of, and if you have to you can step on the straps without any worry of damaging them. They can be purchased already attached to a pair of pedals (the straps can't be mounted to some pedals, most notably plastic ones) or separately, in pairs.

When you're ready to rack up some serious mileage, you should consider some type of aerodynamic handlebar. Shown here is the Syntace C2 Clip Ultralite aerobar. This handlebar attachment is just the thing you need for hammering along lengthy sections of asphalt. It allows you to assume a comfortable aerodynamic tuck and stretches you out to relieve pressure on your arms and wrists. It also reduces back strain.

Bar ends give mountain bikers alternative hand positions for riding up hills and on flat sections (where immediate access to the brake levers is not important). Shown here are Onza's Raw Bars.

Have a seat! - The SDG Comp Ti seat features titanium rails and a Kevlar cover (the stuff used in bulletproof vest construction). This is a very lightweight, narrow seat. You might think a narrow seat would be tortuously uncomfortable, but this isn't necessarily so. Narrow seats are preferred by many riders because they reduce chafing to the inner thighs. (Note: SDG stands for *Speed Defies Gravity*.)

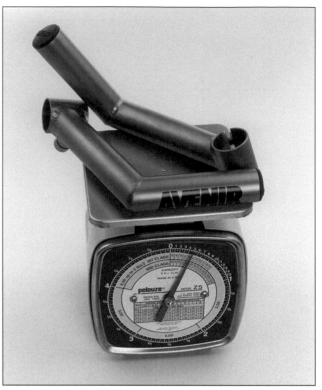

The recycling craze has hit the cycling industry, and rightly so. Shouldn't your environmentally friendly form of transportation/recreation be outfitted with components that have taken a minimal toll on the environment? The people at Pedro's think so, and manufacture water bottle cages and grips made from recycled materials. The bottle cages are formed from 100-percent recycled plastic milk containers, thus the name "Milk Cage." The grips are made from 65-percent recycled rubber products.

Put your bike on a diet! If you get caught up in the weight reduction craze, you'll probably start eyeing titanium parts. Just about every bike part you can think of is available in this space-age material. Titanium is very strong and incredibly light. It's also incredibly expensive. Shown here are Avenir's Team Stiks bar ends.

What's a Chill Pill? Glad you asked. It's a pill-shaped device that connects your brake cable to a straddle cable between your cantilever brake arms. Therefore, it helps you slow down, or "chill!" Unlike a cable carrier in a typical link-wire cantilever brake setup, these Chill Pills by Onza are self-centering, which means brake setup is simplified, and the chance of one brake pad dragging on the rim is eliminated.

Pedro's also makes these tire levers out of 100-percent recycled milk containers.

Upgrading from your present, worn-out dual-purpose treads to a pair of aggressive knobbies will make your bike feel like a completely different machine. Shown here are Onza's Rail and Honch. These tires are designed to provide the ultimate grip in hardpack and sandy soil as well as muddy conditions. With tires like these you'll probably surprise yourself with your new cornering and climbing abilities!

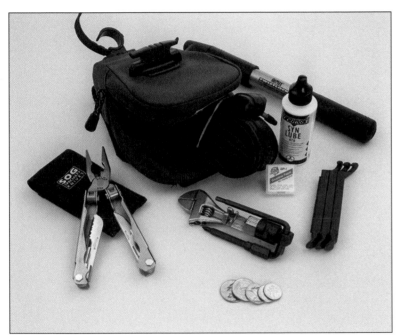

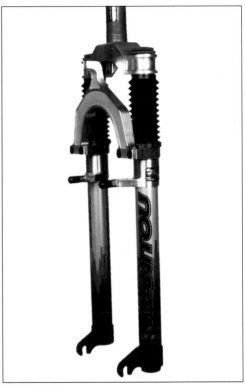

So you want to go faster? Replace your rigid fork with a suspension fork. If you do much off-road riding you'll eventually reach the point where you'll wish you could keep up with the other riders on the trail. If you have a rigid fork, keep wishing! There's no way you're going to keep up with a rider with skills comparable to your own but who has a suspension fork. As he or she glides over ruts and bumps, picking the fast lines through the turns and being able to maintain a higher speed through those turns (because he/she's running higher tire pressures, which enables the tires to "bite" better), you'll be hanging on, barely in control and chewing on the fillings that are falling out of your molars.

What you should take with you - Don't be a burden on others; instead, be as self-sufficient as possible and always carry the necessities. These include a water bottle or two (not shown), a spare tube, a patch kit (shown here is Park Tool's Glueless Patch Kit), a pump, tire levers, a multi-tool (shown here is the Cool Tool) and some change, just in case you have to make a telephone call. The SOG Multi-tool on the left is another handy item to bring, and it's wise to pack a small container of chain lube, especially on long treks. Zip-ties and lengths of wire (not shown) can also get you out of a jam. You should also take at least one of some kind of energy bar (not shown). All of this stuff (except for the water bottle, of course) will fit nicely into a seat pack like this Cannondale Creme de Comp.

By carrying all of the items you feel are necessary to make repairs, you won't have to rely on others to carry this extra weight for you. Plus, you may be able to help somebody else who hasn't yet learned this lesson.

Upgrading to a suspension fork makes so much difference you won't believe it. Shown here is the Answer Manitou EFC (elastomer fluid control). Suspension forks like this one only weigh a little more than a conventional fork, and more than make up for their weight in performance.

What you should have in your shop - If you're serious about maintaining and repairing your bike, you'll want to invest in some bike-specific tools. Most cyclists begin by struggling with regular automotive-style tools until they just can't stand it anymore, then start purchasing bike tools, a few at a time as they are needed. Then they realize that they should have made this investment in the first place! The tools shown here are made by Park Tool Company, and represent a sampling of the more commonly needed tools for bike repair.

Using the proper tools greatly simplifies any maintenance or repair procedure and also reduces the chance of damaging expensive components. These Park tools are of very high quality, are relatively inexpensive, can be found at most bike shops and make working on your bike a pleasure instead of a pain.

Another recommended addition to your workshop is a repair stand of some sort. The one shown here is by Park Tool Company and has a clamp which quickly secures the bike with the throw of a lever. The clamp head also rotates 360-degrees. The tray, available separately, is handy for holding tools and small parts. Once you use a repair stand like this you'll wonder why you suffered so long without one!

Yet another important addition to your shop - degreasers, lubes and cleaners. The products shown here, made by Pedro's, are formulated just for bicycles. Don't defile your bike with automotive wheel bearing grease in your bearings or engine oil on your chain - use the *proper* lubricants. Why use solvents that are harmful to your skin and nasal passages when you can use a degreaser that smells good, works good and is easy on the environment?

These products, just like using proper bicycle tools, will make working on your bike a fun experience instead of a miserable one.

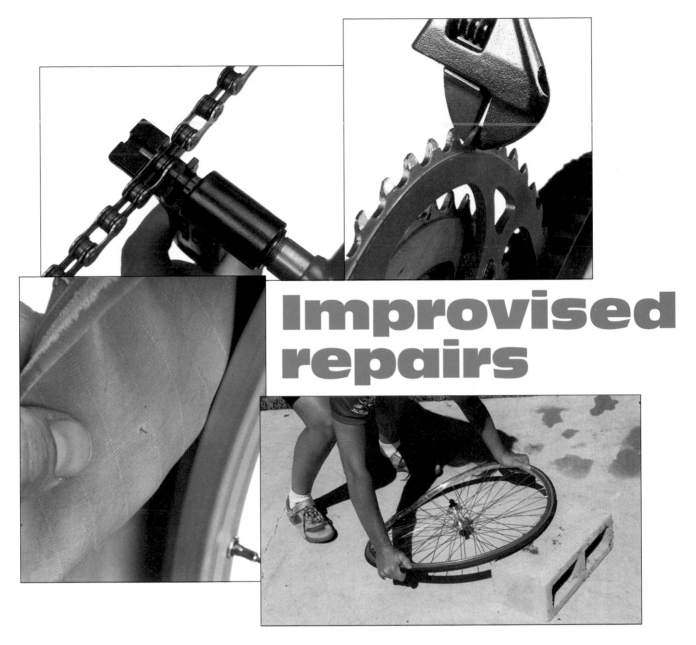

Improvised repairs

Even though you may carry all of the tools and spares you're supposed to, there still may come a time when you have a serious breakdown miles from home or the nearest telephone. At first, things may seem pretty hopeless, and you may think there's nothing you can do but walk or carry your bike back to civilization.

Before you start walking, sit down and think over the situation. Short of a collapsed wheel or a broken frame there's not much that you can't fix with a little creative engineering and readily available materials. Sure the ride back home may be slow going, but it's better than pushing your bike for miles.

Flat tire

This is by far the most common malady that is likely to force you to rest awhile. If the tube is simply punctured by a thorn, nail or the like, follow the procedure described in Chapter 4 to mend it. If the damage is more severe, such as a gash or a large hole that a patch won't cover, cut the tube at the damaged area and tie a knot in each end. Or, if you have two zip-ties, cinch them down as tight as you can on either side of the tear. Stuff the tube back into the tire and fill the section between the ends of the tube (or around the zip-ties) with weeds, sod or a couple of rolled-up T-shirts. Remount the

tire, inflate it and continue on your way. The ride will be bumpy, but the rim will be protected if you use enough filler material.

No tire levers?

If you have a flat tire but forgot to bring your tire levers, remove the quick-release skewers from your hubs and pry the tire off with the levers.

Torn sidewall

Aggressive riding can yield unpleasant results sometimes. Torn sidewalls usually happen while riding hard over rocky terrain, or after a puncture has occurred and the tire deflates. If you can re-

pair or replace the tube you should then patch up the gash in the tire sidewall with anything strong enough to keep the tube from herniating out through the hole. Dollar bills, thick leaves, a business card, duct tape or a piece of inner tube will usually suffice.

Broken rear derailleur

The rear derailleur is an especially vulnerable component. It's almost sure to get bent or broken if you lay it over on the right side, and roots or low tree branches can catch on it as you ride by, which could even tear it off the frame. If this happens, take your chain tool and remove as many links of the chain as necessary to run the chain around the middle chainring (triple-ring cranksets) or the small chainring (double-ring cranksets) and one of the middle sprockets at the rear. If you can, unbolt the derailleur and store it in your pack so it doesn't flop around as you ride.

Broken chain

If you discover a weak link in your chain you can probably get away with removing the broken portion with your chain tool and rejoining the chain; most chains are long enough to allow you to do this, but you may have to avoid using the large chainring or the biggest sprocket. If you don't have a chain tool (shame on you) join the chain with a piece of wire, if you can find one - coat hanger wire is just about the right size. Bend the ends of the wire back and wrap a piece of tape around the repair to keep the wire in place. The drawback to this method is that you'll have to place the repaired section along the bottom run of the chain and ratchet the pedals back and forth to prevent the repaired area from traveling around the chainring or rear sprockets.

Snapped shift cable

Shift cables rarely fail, but if one does you can rejoin the cable using just about anything long enough to span the gap after the ends of the cable have been tied to it; a flattened soda can with holes punched in each end, a strip of wood, a couple of zip-ties linked together, or even your wristwatch. You'll have to adjust the slack out of the cable to provide useable shifting.

If your improvised cable repair gives you unsatisfactory results, shorten the chain and run your bike as a one-speed.

Broken brake straddle cable or link wire

Another rare occurrence, but one that is not out of the question. Shoelaces, zip-ties and even a bent spare spoke can take the place of the cable in an emergency. You'll need to adjust the main brake cable after the temporary repair is made.

Bent wheels

Bent wheels or squared rims and rims with dings or bulges can usually be repaired by applying force in the opposite direction of the bend. Refer to Chapter 4 for rim repair methods.

Broken handlebar

A broken handlebar is usually the result of a crash or an extremely hard landing from a jump, which will most likely cause a crash. If you're still able to ride after such an occurrence, look around for a stick that will fit snugly inside of the handlebar. Cram it into the part of the bar that is still attached to the bike, then pound the severed portion of the bar onto the stick. Don't expect too much performance, but it will give you something to hang onto.

Bent chainrings

Bent chainrings can be straightened using an adjustable wrench as a lever. The most common damage to chainrings is a bent tooth on the large chainring caused by contact with an obstacle that the bike high-centered on. The Cool Tool (see Chapter 13) is an excellent prescription for curing this ailment.

Broken freewheel

All of your pedaling power is ultimately transferred to the wheel through two little pawls in the freewheel or freehub. If these pawls become sticky or decide to give up the ghost, your hub will freewheel in both directions. Many riders would concede at this point and resort to walking to the nearest pay phone. All you need to do is secure the freewheel or freehub to the wheel; this can be done by zip-tying the largest rear sprocket to the spokes. If you don't have any zip-ties, remove the straps from your toe clips (if you use them) and thread them though the large sprocket and around the spokes, cinching them down as tight as possible. Even shoelaces will work.

Remember, if you do this you won't be able to coast because you have no freewheel.

Broken seat

A seat that won't stay attached to its rails can be secured with duct tape or tied into place with strips of material, such as a torn-up T-shirt. If this is not an option, remove the seat post and ride the rest of the way standing up!

Broken pedal

The most likely candidate for this affliction is a plastic pedal. These pedals can shatter if they catch on an immovable object at speed. if the pedal spindle is still intact you can tape or wire a piece of wood to the spindle to provide a platform for your foot.

Missing crank bolt

You probably won't have to worry about this disorder if you properly maintain your bike as outlined in Chapter 2. However, if your crank arm falls off while you're out on a ride, remove the bolt from the opposite crank arm (you have a Cool Tool, right?), re-mount the detached crank arm and install the bolt, tightening it securely. Now, if you have a Cool Tool, take the emergency crank bolt (the threaded portion of the chain tool) and install it into the crank arm that you removed the bolt from. It should provide enough force to prevent the already-tight crank arm from coming loose.

Bolts so tight that you can't loosen them

If you encounter a bolt that you just can't loosen, remove the seat post from your frame and slip the post over the wrench, using it as a "cheater pipe" to increase your leverage.

Glossary

Adjustable cup - The left-side cup in the bottom bracket, which can be screwed in or out to adjust the bottom bracket bearings. It's also the cup to remove when overhauling the bottom bracket.

Aheadset - A headset design that uses a threadless steerer tube. The steerer tube is secured in the headset bearings by the stem.

Anti-seize - A type of grease laced with lead particles, used to prevent two components from corroding together. Mainly used on threaded fasteners - don't use it in bearings (it isn't a high-speed lubricant).

Axle - The threaded shaft that passes through the center of the hub that the wheel rotates on. Sometimes used to refer to the bottom bracket spindle.

Axle nut - The nut that threads onto the axle and holds the wheel to the fork or frame.

Axle protrusion - The distance between the bearing cone adjuster locknut on the axle to the end of the axle.

B-tension screw - The screw at the rear of a Shimano derailleur that adjusts the distance between the derailleur guide wheel and the rear sprockets.

Bar ends - Extensions that bolt onto the ends of a mountain bike handlebar and offer the rider different hand positions. Designed primarily for climbing hills and for use on long stretches of road or trail where the brakes aren't needed.

Bead - The part of a clincher tire that you sometimes have to lever up over the rim during installation. Usually reinforced with wire or Kevlar strands.

Bead seat - The part of the rim where the bead of a clincher tire seats.

Bottom bracket - The bearing assembly that the crank arms are attached to.

Bottom bracket shell - The part of the frame that the bottom bracket is housed in.

Bottom bracket spindle - The shaft that the crank arms attach to and the bottom bracket bearings support. Also referred to as the bottom bracket axle.

Brake block - Another term for *brake pad*.

Brake centering - Adjusting the brake so both pads are equidistant from the rim while at rest and contact the rim at the same time when the brake is applied.

Brake pad - The rubber part of the brake that presses against the rim when the brakes are applied, creating friction.

Brake pad toe-in - The difference in distance between the ends of the brake pad and the rim. The trailing end of the pad (in relation to wheel rotation) should contact the rim slightly before the leading end.

Brake release (or quick release) - A lever or button that can be disengaged to allow the brake pads to spread apart, making wheel removal easier.

Braze-ons - Small mounting bosses on a bike frame for attaching water bottle cages, racks, shifters, derailleurs, brake arms, etc., attached by the process of brazing.

Butted spoke - A spoke that is thicker at the ends than in the middle.

Butted tubing - Frame tubing that is thicker at the ends than in the middle, but has the same outside diameter along its length. This places more material at the stress points and eliminates material in the middle, which makes for lighter tubing.

Cable - A control mechanism, composed of an inner cable (stranded wire) and an outer casing, used for operating derailleurs and brakes.

Cable carrier - The component in a link-wire cantilever brake system that joins the brake cable going to one brake arm with the link wire that goes to the other arm.

Cable hanger - A mounting boss that holds a cable casing but lets the inner cable pass through.

Cadence - Pedaling rpm (revolutions per minute).

Cage - 1. On the rear derailleur, the two plates that hold the tension and guide wheels. 2. On the front derailleur, the two parallel plates that move the chain from chainring-to-chainring. 3. A frame-mounted water bottle holder. 4. Ball bearing retainer.

Calipers - The parts of a brake that the cable pulls on, through which force is

transmitted to push the brake pads against the rim. Also called brake arms.

Cantilever brake - A brake with two caliper arms, each one being mounted on opposite sides of the frame or fork. The most common type of brake found on mountain bikes.

Cartridge bottom bracket - A self-contained, non-serviceable bottom bracket axle and bearing assembly.

Center-pull brake - A brake design in which the caliper arms pivot on a common mount attached to the frame or fork, each arm being attached by a straddle cable which the main brake cable pulls.

Chain breaker - A tool used for driving a rivet out of a chain to separate it, and then driving it back in again to rejoin the chain.

Chain rivet - The pins of a chain that connect the individual links.

Chain roller - The round part between the plates of a chain that engage between the teeth of the sprockets and chainrings.

Chain stretch - The amount a chain "grows" as the rivets and rollers wear out.

Chain whip - A tool used for unscrewing the small sprocket to disassemble a freewheel, and also used to prevent a freehub from turning while unscrewing the lockring. Composed of a metal bar, a short length of chain to grip the sprocket and a longer length of chain which wraps around the sprocket to pull on it.

Chainguard - A protective covering over the chain and chainrings, designed primarily to keep fingers and clothing from getting caught in the chain.

Chainring - The large sprocket(s) on a crankset which pulls on the chain as the cranks are turned. Sometimes referred to as a chainwheel.

Chainstays - The parts of a frame that make up the bottom portion of the rear triangle; the two tubes that travel between the bottom bracket and the rear wheel dropouts.

Chainwheel - See *Chainring*.

Clincher - The common term used to describe any bike tire that uses a separate inner tube.

Clipless pedal - A type of pedal that incorporates a foot retention system that doesn't use straps.

Cogs - Another term for the rear sprockets.

Cone - The inner race of a ball-type bearing assembly. Found on axles and some bottom brackets.

Crank arm - The part of a crankset that connects the pedal to the bottom bracket.

Crank puller - A tool required to remove the crank arms from the bottom bracket spindle.

Crankset - The components that work together to pull the chain; comprised of the bottom bracket, crank arms and chainring(s).

Cup - The outer race of a ball-type bearing assembly. Found on bottom brackets and headsets. (On axle bearings the cup is integral with the hub.)

Derailleur - The cable-actuated mechanism used for shifting the chain from one sprocket or chainring to another.

Derailleur chain - Type of chain designed for use with derailleur shifting systems.

Derailleur hanger - The protrusion on the rear-wheel dropout to which the derailleur mounts.

Dish - The position of the hub in relation to the rim. A wheel whose hub flanges protrude equidistant from each side of the rim has zero dish. Rear wheels on multi-speed bikes must have a certain amount of dish to make room for the freewheel or freehub sprockets.

Down tube - The part of the frame that travels from the head tube to the bottom bracket; it forms the bottom part of the front triangle.

Drop bars - Typical handlebars found on road bikes that curve down from the tops of the bars.

Dropouts - The machined plates with slots that a wheel axle fits into; also the slots themselves.

Ferrule - The metal cap on the end of a cable casing.

Fixed cup - The cup of an adjustable bottom bracket assembly that is threaded into the right-hand side of the frame.

Fork - The tubes that hold the front wheel to the bike.

Fork crown - The part of a fork that attaches the fork blades or tubes to the steerer tube.

Fourth-hand tool - A tool used for pulling cables tight.

Freehub - A ratcheting mechanism to which the rear sprockets mount, also incorporating the drive-side axle bearing.

Freewheel - A ratcheting mechanism to which the rear sprockets mount, independent of the wheel axle bearings.

Freewheel remover - A special tool used for removing a freewheel.

Friction shifters - Non-index type shift levers that rely on friction to hold the derailleur in position.

Front triangle - The front structural part of the frame, comprised of the top tube, seat tube, head tube and down tube.

Gooseneck - Another term for the *stem*.

GripShift - A type of index shifter that changes gears by rotating the innermost part of the handgrip.

Guide wheel - The upper wheel of a rear derailleur - it moves the chain from one sprocket to another.

"H" screw - The adjustment screw on a derailleur that sets the limit of travel towards the high gear (big chainring up front, small sprocket at the rear). When adjusted correctly it prevents the chain from jumping off between the small sprocket and the frame (rear) or off the large chainring (front).

Head tube - The part of the frame that the fork steerer tube passes through.

Headset - The bearings that support the fork steerer tube.

Hub - The center portion of the wheel, containing the axle and bearings.

Hyperglide chain - Derailleur chain designed for use with Shimano Hyperglide shifting systems, with specially shaped plates to provide quick, smooth shifting. Requires a special replacement rivet if separated.

Idler wheels - Another term for the guide and tension wheels of the rear derailleur.

Index shifters - Shifters that change gears with a click of the lever.

Indexed steering - "Notchy" steering caused by a worn-out headset.

Jockey wheels - Another term for the guide and tension wheels of the rear derailleur.

"L" screw - The adjustment screw on a derailleur that sets the limit of travel towards the low gear (big sprocket on the rear, small chainring on the front). When adjusted correctly it prevents the chain from jumping off the big rear sprocket and tearing out spokes, or from coming off the small front chainring and landing on the bottom bracket shell.

Link-wire cantilever brake - A cantilever brake setup where the main cable connects to one cantilever arm and the other arm is connected to the main cable by a shorter cable and cable carrier.

Locknut - A nut that tightens up against an adjuster nut to prevent it from moving.

Lockring - The ring nut that threads over the left side bottom bracket bearing cup and locks it to the bottom bracket shell when tightened.

Lugs - Castings with external metal tubes into which frame tubes are brazed or glued.

Main triangle - See *Front triangle*.

Master link - A link of chain that can be separated without having to drive out a rivet.

Narrow chain - Derailleur chain with a narrower width than standard derailleur chain. Most require a special replacement pin if separated.

Nipples - The nuts that fit through holes in the rim and thread onto the ends of the spokes.

Presta valve - A type of tire tube valve that has a small nut on top that must be loosened to add or release air.

Quick-release - A device that allows rapid detachment or adjustment of a component. Found on some wheels and seat binder bolts.

Quick-release skewer - The thin rod that passes through the center of a hollow axle.

Race - The part of a bearing assembly that the bearing balls or rollers contact.

Rear triangle - The rear structural part of the frame, made up of the seat stays, chain stays and seat tube.

Retainer - The plastic or pressed metal cage that holds ball bearings a specified distance from each other.

Rim - The outer portion of the wheel that the tire fits on.

Rim strip - A rubber liner that encircles the rim and covers the spoke nipples to prevent them from damaging the tube.

Rim tape - Cloth adhesive tape that performs the same function as a rim strip.

Saddle - Another term used for a bicycle seat.

Schrader valve - An automotive-type tire valve.

Seal - A synthetic rubber boot or flange that fits over a bearing to keep contaminants out.

Seat post - The tube that the seat mounts on.

Seat stays - The tubes of a frame that span the distance between the seat tube and the rear dropouts.

Seat tube - The vertical part of the frame that forms the rear of the front triangle, running between the bottom bracket and the top tube.

Sew-up tire - A tire that has it's tube stitched inside; must be glued to the rim.

Skewer - See *Quick-release skewer*.

Spider - The part of the right-side crank arm that the chainrings attach to.

Spin - To pedal at a high cadence.

Spindle - The part of a bottom bracket that the crank arms attach to.

Spoke - The wires that extend from the hub to the rim.

Spoke guard - A plate, made from plastic or metal, which prevents the chain from tearing out the drive-side spokes on the rear wheel if the chain jumps off the largest rear sprocket.

Spoke nipples - See *Nipples*.

Spoke wrench - A wrench used to turn spoke nipples.

Sprocket - A gear on the rear wheel.

Steerer tube - The part of the fork that passes through the head tube of the frame and is supported by the headset bearings.

Stem - The part that connects the handlebar to the fork steerer tube.

Stem binder bolt - The bolt in the center of a conventional stem that pulls up on a wedge when tightened, fixing the stem's position in the fork steerer tube.

Straddle cable - A cable that attaches one brake arm to another. Used in straddle-cable cantilever brakes and center-pull brakes.

Straddle-cable cantilever brake - A cantilever brake setup where the main cable connects to a yoke, which connects to a cable running between the two cantilever arms.

Tension wheel - The lower wheel of a rear derailleur - it maintains tension on the bottom run of the chain.

Third-hand tool - A tool that squeezes the brake pads against the rim to ease cable adjustment.

Tire lever - A small plastic lever used to pry a tire off of the rim. Usually more than one is required.

Toe clip - A foot retention system mounted on the pedal, consisting of a metal or plastic cage that covers the front part of the foot, sometimes secured at the rear by a strap that tightens over the center part of the foot.

Top tube - The upper part of the front triangle, connected to the head tube and the seat tube.

Truing stand - A fixture that is used to true-up wheels.

Trueness - The straightness, both laterally and axially, of a wheel as it rotates.

Tubular - See *Sew-up tire*.

U-brake - A type of brake that is similar to a cross between a center-pull brake and a cantilever brake.

Valve stem - The part of an inner tube that protrudes through the rim that air is added to.

Wheel dish - See *Dish*.

Sourcelist

Access Marketing
P.O. Box 3109
Shell Beach
*Slime tire sealant and self-healing
tubes*

AMP Research
1855 Laguna Canyon Rd.
Laguna Beach, CA 92651
*Full-suspension mountain bike frames,
forks, disc brakes*

Answer Products, Inc.
27460 Avenue Scott
Valencia, CA 91355
*Manitou suspension forks, other high-
performance mountain bike
components, clothing*

Anti-Gravity, Inc.
249 South Hwy. 101 #404
Solana Beach, CA 92057-1807
Suspension forks

Azonic
9555 Owensmouth Ave.
Chatsworth, CA 91311
Mountain bike frames and components

Barnett Bicycle Institute
2755 Ore Mill Dr., #14B
Colorado Springs, CO 80904
Bicycle repair courses

Bell Sports
160 Knowles Dr.
Los Gatos, CA 95030
Helmet manufacturer

Bicycle Parts Pacific
P.O. Box 4250
Grand Junction, CO 81502
Powergrip pedals and straps

Bike Nashbar
4111 Simon Rd.
Youngstown, OH 44512-1343
Tel. 1-800-NASHBAR
*Mail order bikes, parts, accessories
and clothing*

Blackburn
160 Knowles Dr.
Los Gatos, CA 95030
Manufacturer of bicycle accessories

Cat Eye Electronics
1705 14th St. #115
Boulder, CO 80302
Cycle computers

Cannondale Corporation
9 Brookside Place, P.O. Box 122
Georgetown, CT 06829-0122
*Manufacturer of aluminum-framed
bicycles. Also manufacture bike parts
and accessories.*

Cook Bros. Racing
1983 Willow Road
Arroyo Grande, CA 93420
*Makers of cranksets and bottom
brackets*

Cool Tool
13524 Autumn Lane
Chico, CA 95926
*Manufacturer of the Cool Tool and
other multi-tools. Also the home of
Retrotec bicycles.*

Craig Metalcraft, Inc.
4724 West Rice
Chicago, IL 60651
*Superlink II chain link (can be
separated without a chain tool)*

Dia-Compe
Box 798, 355 Cane Creek Road
Fletcher, NC 28732
Manufacturer of bicycle components

Foes Fab
2660 Deodar Circle
Pasadena, CA 91107
Full-suspension mountain bike frames

Fox
15850 Concord Circle
Concord Circle
*Morgan Hill, CA 95037
Mountain biking apparel*

Giro Sport Design
380 Encinal St.
Santa Cruz, CA 95060
Helmets, Pocketshop multi-tool

GT Bicycles Inc.
3100 W. Segerstrom Ave.
Santa Ana, CA 92704
*Manufacturer of GT bicycles and
components*

Headland Bicycle Accessories
P.O. Box 2641
San Rafael, CA 94912
Utility-X rack and other accesssories

Innovations in Cycling
2700 E. Bilby Road
Tucson, AZ 85706
Racin'flate tire inflators

**International Mountain
Bicycling Association (IMBA)**
P.O. Box 7578
Boulder, CO 80306
*Promoters of enviromentally sound,
socially responsible mountain biking
(with the goal of keeping trails open)*

Iron Horse USA
11 Constance Court
Hauppauge, NY 11788
Manufacturer of Iron Horse mountain bikes

Litespeed Titanium
P.O. Box 22666
Chattanooga, TN 37422
Manufacturer of titanium-framed bicycles

Marzocchi Suspension Center
28150 Avenue Crocker, Suite 221
Valencia, CA 91355
Suspension forks

Mavic, Inc.
207 Carter Dr.
West Chester, PA 19382
Bicycle rim manufacturer

Nightsun Performance Lighting
396 West Washington Blvd. #600
Pasadena, CA 91103
Rechargeable lighting systems

Onza
1666 9th Street
Santa Monica, CA 90404
High-performance mountain bike components

Parkpre USA
5245 Kazuko Court
Moorpark, CA 93021
Manufacturer of Parkpre bicycles

Park Tool Company
3535 International Drive
St. Paul, MN 55110
High-quality bicycle tools

Pedro's
P.O. Box 3532
Newport, RI 02840-0991
Manufacturer of environmentally friendly degreasers, lubricants, and components made from recycled materials

Precision Billet
9437 Wheatlands Ct., Ste. C
Santee, CA 92071
Mountain bike parts machined from billet aluminum

Profile Racing
5290 95th St. N.
St. Petersburg, Fl. 33708
CNC machined cranksets, chainrings

Qranc USA
P.O. Box 1751 - 40298 Big Bear Blvd.
Big Bear Lake, CA 92315-1751
Mountain bike components

Race Face
1318 Cliveden Ave.
Annacis Park
Delta, British Columbia V3M 6G4
High-performance mountain bike parts

Ringlé Components, Inc.
101 Walters Ave.
Trenton, NJ 08638
Aluminum mountain bike hubs, seatposts, stems, quick releases, etc.

Rock Shox
Tel. 408-435-7469
Suspension fork manufacturer

Sachs Bicycle components
22445 E. LaPalma Ave., Ste. J
Yorba Linda, CA 92687
Manufacturer of bicycle components

Scott USA
Boulder, CO
Tel. 1-800-292-5875
High-performance bikes and accessories

SDG USA (Speed Defies Gravity)
212 Technology Suite #C
Irvine, CA 92718
High-performance seats

Shimano American Corporation
Irvine, CA
1-800-423-2420
Worlds largest manufacturer of bicycle components

Specialized
15130 Concord Circle
Morgan Hill, CA 95037-5493
Manufacturer of bicycles and components

SRAM Corp.
Chicago, IL
Tel. 312-664-8800
GripShift shifters

Syntace USA
2522 Chambers Road, Ste. 110
Tustin, CA 92680
Makers of handlebars, aerobars, stems, bar ends and other components

Tange USA Corporation
280 N. Westlake Blvd., Ste. 210
Westlake Village, CA 91362
Suspension forks, bicycle frame tubing

Todson, Inc.
14 Connor Lane
Deer Park, NY 11729
Zefal pumps

Trek Bicycle Corporation
801 West Madison Street
P.O. Box 183
Waterloo, WI 53594
Manufacturer of Trek bicycles and accessories

Troy Lee Designs
1821 Wild Turkey Cir.
Corona, CA 91720
Riding attire, packs, visors, etc.

Velimpex Marketing, Inc.
P.O. Box 272552
Ft. Collins, CO 80527-2552
High-performance seats

Vivo
11 Keswick Lane
Plainview, NY 11803
Grunge Guard Derailleur Boot

Western States Imports
Tel. (805) 484-4450
Diamond Back bicylces and Avenir accessories

W.L. Gore and Associates, Inc.
1505 N. Fourth Street
Flagstaff, AZ 86003
RideOn Hyperformance cable systems

Index